The first Viet Cong spider hole opened under a woven winnowing mat. The wounded enemy soldier popped up and took careful aim at a trooper bringing up the first squad's flank. *Blam! Blaam! Blaam!* The SKS semiautomatic rifle spit. The young Marine on the flank faltered, then pitched forward—another "new guy," this one had lasted less than a month. It was the seasoned troopers like Lafley, Burns, Ybarra, and Jessmore who were tough to kill—or just damn lucky.

Burns wheeled in the street to face a row of huts, then called to Lafley. "Watch my back. I'm going into that hut to see what's left alive." He entered the smoking frame of the doorway. Screams became audible as the staccato rhythm of Burns's rifle silenced the noise. Burns emerged wearing a Viet Cong pith helmet, the red star shining in the front. . . .

OPERATION TUSCALOOSA

2nd Battalion, 5th Marines, at An Hoa, 1967

Sgt. John J. Culbertson, U.S.M.C.

IVY BOOKS • NEW YORK

Copyright © 1997 by John J. Culbertson

All rights reserved under International and Pan-American Copyright Conventions. Published in the United States by Ballantine Books, a division of Random House, Inc., New York, and simultaneously in Canada by Random House of Canada Limited, Toronto.

http://www.randomhouse.com

Library of Congress Catalog Card Number: 96-95464

ISBN 0-8041-1565-6

Printed in Canada

First Edition: June 1997

10   9   8   7   6

IN MEMORIAM

The heroes of the Second Battalion, Fifth Marine Regiment, First Marine Division who gave their lives for their brothers on January 26, 1967. Trapped on a sandbar, they made the final sacrifice for God, Country, and Corps. May their hearts be at rest with our Lord, who drew up their souls in powerful arms to the safety of His heaven.

Greater love hath no man than this, that a man lay down his life for his friends.

Name	Rank	Serial Number
David Jamison	PFC	2168658
William F. Kranz, Jr.	PFC	2153926
Allan Guinn	PFC	2184039
Joseph R. Wallen	L.Cpl.	2132183
Douglas L. Tracy	Cpl.	2099098
James P. Bauer	PFC	2273570
James E. Myers	L.Cpl.	2030737
Thomas R. Snaith	L.Cpl.	2105055
Nelson K. Rivers	L.Cpl.	2153759
Dennis W. Baxter	PFC	2169289
Mark E. Robinson	PFC	2270044
Gary T. Fraley	PFC	2210340
Malcolm C. Smith	L.Cpl.	2101537
Richard N. Stansell	PFC	2241539

IN MEMORIAM

Name	Rank	Serial Number
Kirby W. Bradford	PFC	2223944
Thomas J. Carey	Sgt.	2043842
Earl F. Smith	2d Lt.	095344

CONTENTS

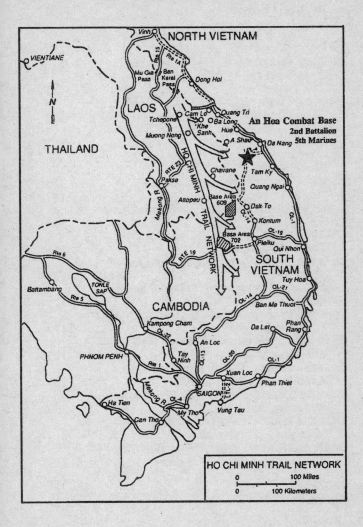

Prologue

In 1966 the First Marine Division was locked in a serious struggle along the DMZ (demilitarized zone) to attempt to halt North Vietnamese infiltration of South Vietnam. The Rockpile, Cam Lo, and Con Thien were all Marine combat bases adapted to provide a jumping-off point for Marine search-and-destroy operations targeted against North Vietnamese army units pushing south. Also, Marine artillery units were deployed to fire H and I (harassment and interdiction) fire missions against the enemy around the clock.

The Marine High Command at III MAF (Third Marine Amphibious Force), Phu Bai (Third Marine Division), and Da Nang (First Marine Division) were dedicating a plan of search-and-destroy operations designed to displace the enemy from his traditional strongholds and then execute a pacification program to bring contested villages under U.S. and Vietnamese allied control.

This account is based on a true series of events involving the Second Battalion, Fifth Marine Regiment, First Marine Division, based in An Hoa, twenty-five miles southwest of the giant Marine base at Da Nang. An Hoa was the westernmost logistical combat base in the Marine TAOR (tactical area of responsibility), called I Corps, or the northernmost of the four sectors of military control in South Vietnam.

In late 1966, the Second Battalion, Fifth Marines (2/5) was encountering constant enemy activity in its area of operations—specifically, the An Hoa basin and the Song Thu Bon and Song Vu Gia valleys to the northwest. Marine planners wanted to create a situation that would draw the enemy (main force Viet Cong led by NVA regulars) into a fixed battle. A strategy was developed to penetrate the Viet Cong base camps by stages, forcing them to defend their territory of operations en masse. This probing would be accomplished by search-and-destroy operations utilizing a larger sweep or killer force to drive out the enemy and a smaller blocking force to channel the enemy's movement. Once hemmed in, the Viet Cong would likely fight if trapped, particularly during daylight hours.

Having the enemy's main body caught between a pair of Marine rifle companies was the best scenario offered by the Marine General Staff's strategy. The General Staff's officers at III MAF knew only too well what the outcome would be if a Viet Cong main force battalion was forced to shoot it out with a pair of Marine rifle companies—or a Marine rifle battalion reinforced with artillery and air support. Nothing could cut an enemy to pieces faster than a "government issue" Marine rifle battalion.

The generals decided that a decisive pitched battle was needed. If necessary, the generals were willing to pay the price of bringing this elusive Viet Cong enemy to his knees with young Marine lives.

PART ONE:
Prelude

CHAPTER ONE

Da Nang, Portal to Quang Nam

My liberty ship landed at the bustling port of Da Nang on December 29, 1966. I disembarked as one of the 2,700 replacements for the First Marine Division. The individual Marines were divided into groups by the attendant personnel officers. Each group made up a replacement platoon that was assigned to a specific infantry or artillery battalion serving in Quang Nam Province, which was the TAOR (tactical area of responsibility) for the First Marine Division as part of III MAF (Marine Amphibious Force).

My particular party of twenty Marines between the ages of eighteen and twenty-one was eager to join the battle against the evils of Communism. We were approached by a mid-thirties major who faced our formation and began: "You men have come to Vietnam to do battle with the heathen, Commie hordes that are our enemies. You will be posted to the Second Battalion of the Fifth Marine Regiment. Two-Five is one of the most storied, highly decorated battalions in the entire Marine Corps. The Second Battalion has distinguished itself as Heartbreakers and Life-Takers from

3

Belleau Wood in World War I to Guadalcanal in World War II, where they beat back the banzai attack of the Japanese Imperial Marines' Ichiki Battalion and killed them with volley fire to a man. In Korea, the Second Battalion formed the backbone of the famed Chosin Reservoir breakout by the First Provisional Marine Brigade under the command of that legendary old bulldog, General "Chesty" Puller. In Vietnam, the Second Battalion has just pulled out of the DMZ [demilitarized zone] at Con Thien and Cam Lo, where it has engaged NVA [North Vietnamese Army] regular units in extremely ferocious combat. You men will be joining the battalion at the An Hoa Combat Base, which is the Marines' westernmost installation in I [pronounced "eye"] Corps and is about twenty-five miles southwest of Da Nang down Highway One."

The major continued his brief sitrep (situation report): "An Hoa is the key logistical facility from which the Marines launch patrols and operational sweeps to clear the surrounding hamlets dotting the Arizona Territory. It contains the hostile and deadly Thu Bon and Vu Gia river valleys. These comprise the major geographical features of the rice paddy basins of the Dai Loc and Duc Duc districts. Within and surrounding the TAOR for Two-Five there have been approximately twenty-four enemy infantry and support battalions operating in Quang Nam Province. We have been actively engaging them with the assistance of the Second Korean Marine Brigade [Blue Dragons], based at Hoi An. Nineteen sixty-seven will be the year we drive Charlie [Victor Charlie—Viet Cong guerrillas] from his river-based sanctuaries and exterminate him in the open field.

"Any of you men who are not prepared to fight for your country have joined the wrong outfit. Second Battalion, Fifth Marines is a combat unit. Line outfits [infantry battalions] kick ass and take names. I am charged with the onerous responsibility of affording young men the opportunity to collect some scalps. Do not fail your Marine Corps! Do not fail God Almighty, who hates the heathen Communists. Do not fail yourselves or the task for which you became Marines. Chesty Puller is watching all of us! God bless you men. Board the six-by trucks to my rear. Check all your gear. That is all."

"Well, shit! Welcome to Vietnam, you all. I'm glad to see we're going to be pulling some easy duty for the next thirteen months. Jesus! Second Battalion, Fifth Marines! That's just great! I hope everyone spelled his next of kin clearly on the insurance form back at [Camp] Pendleton."

A burly sergeant in jungle utilities walked up to our despairing mob and yelled, "Knock off the bullshit, grab your seabags, and mount the vehicles. I ain't about to drive this bomb-infested highway to no An Hoa in the dark. Let's move it!"

The engines of the two olive drab U.S.M.C. three-axle main transport trucks coughed to life. We loaded our seabags and gear into the two trucks with ten men in each rear bed. There were two Motor T (motor transport) Marines in the cab of each vehicle. The shotgun Motor T Marines were armed with the standard combat rifle, the M-14, and twenty-round magazines. It finally dawned on all of us that this trip was not practice or a training mission. This was the real thing. Two other Motor T Marines carried bulky machine guns, Browning Air-Cooled Caliber .50's with attached metal ammunition boxes containing two hundred rounds of ammunition. One machine gun was placed in the right front mounting pylon in each truck bed. The gunner could stand comfortably in the bed of the six-by-six and command a 180-degree field of fire from left to right, covering his direct front, sweeping the territory ahead of the vehicle and shooting over the top of the cab's canvas top. Extra metal boxes of ammo were passed up to the gun mount. I felt better about this machine gun business. In ITR (Infantry Training Regiment), after boot camp, we'd fired the .50-caliber machine guns. They cycled at around 450 RPM (rounds per minute), which was sluggish compared to the standard infantry M-60 7.62mm machine gun. But the Browning .50-caliber would really reach out and grab your ass. I mean, at two thousand yards it would tear a man in two. Yeah, I felt a lot better about having those two guns on board.

The trucks started to roll, and one of the drivers leaned out the right truck door and instructed, "One of you Marines man each of the guns. Pull the cocking lever to the rear to arm the weapon. Do not fire unless fired upon. If we are fired upon, I will return fire first, then you will engage the enemy by firing in short bursts toward my bullet strike. Is that clear!"

I could already see myself behind that big, nasty .50, chewing up some Commie butt.

We passed though the Da Nang air base with its rows of Quonset huts and sentry towers. We passed sandbagged bunkers at the edge of the dirt road and crossed double-skirted concertina-wired defenses manned by Marine MPs at banded black-and-white road-crossing barriers prohibiting our exit from the Da Nang base perimeter. The Marine guards halted our truck and inspected the driver's trip manifest.

"Where are you boys headed on a nice afternoon like this, Corporal?"

"We're transporting these replacements down Highway One to An Hoa Combat Base."

"Hold your position, Corporal, we've got a couple of medical personnel and some medical supplies going along with you. You will also have an M-60 and an Ontos* from First Tanks to run point and trail for your convoy. Give 'em about fifteen minutes to form up. Also, we've got some bandoliers of ball ammo for your passengers. These guys are all oh-threes [0311 is the Military Occupational Specialty designation for Marine infantry], aren't they?"

"No idea about the MOS situation. The Six [Motor T captain] just told us to haul this live meat down to the grinder at An Hoa. Hey, are all you assholes oh-threes or what?"

"Yeah, man, we all too stupid to be anything else besides oh-three-one-one. Why, do you guys need another driver? I'm a hell of a clutch man myself,"

Ontos is Greek for "the thing," and in the Marines it designated a six-barreled antitank vehicle. The Ontos was fairly small but delivered a blinding backblast when fired. It seemed as punishing to the shooters as the shootees.

was offered from the back of the lead truck by a giant Marine from Louisiana.

As soon as the trucks carrying the medical personnel and supplies formed up behind us, the MP sergeant said, "I'm passing out two magazines and two bandoliers of ammo per Marine. Get your magazines fully charged and insert one into your weapon without chambering a live round. I repeat, without locking and loading. You will take your firing instructions from the driver or assistant driver. Highway One is bordered by many villages along the route to An Hoa. Remember, we are here to kill the fucking Communists, not the local villagers. That is all! Have a safe trip."

The barricade was raised and the convoy lurched across the small bridge and picked up speed down the winding red dirt road that led us into the Vietnamese countryside and into harm's way.

CHAPTER TWO

Land of the Rice Paddy Daddy

The convoy was led by an Ontos. The Marine hybrid fast attack, tracked ambush vehicle was capable of speeds exceeding thirty miles per hour. The light-weight yet fully armored Ontos sported six 106mm recoilless rifles mounted in triangles of three to each side of the armored battle hull. The capability of firing a six-gun fusillade at near-point-blank range gave the Ontos formidable firepower. However, the loader had to exit the rear of the vehicle to reload. But the Ontos's relatively diminutive size, great speed, and maneuver-ability made it the perfect point vehicle for a convoy or road sweep. The big six-by double-axle trucks followed their powerful little cousin at distances of about twenty-five meters. All the olive drab monsters churned the red dirt roadbed into a blanket of suspended dust that clung like masks of dried blood to the sweaty faces of the troopers in the open truck beds.

A big M-60 tank brought up the rear of the convoy, following the trucks carrying the medical teams and supplies. The M-60 Main Battle Tank sported a 90mm main cannon and mounted an internal machine gun, as well as a larger caliber-.50 atop the turret. The M-60 was a fearsome weapon on hard roads, but the muddy rice fields that stretched in all directions from Highway One were impassable to the sixty-ton steel monsters.

The little band of Marine vehicles wound its way over hill and dale and passed groups of local villagers and farmers along the roadside. The Vietnamese seemed not to notice the giant olive drab trucks as they churned by the rows of thatched huts. A half mile ahead the Ontos slammed its starboard track to a halt and pivoted hard right, targeting the outlying fields with its array of rifles. The trucks halted one by one and pulled to the edge of the roadbed.

The troops disembarked and were instantly smothered by hordes of children dressed in every imaginable combination of ragged clothing. Their only common trait was their curiosity about the big, grinning Americans: "Hey, Joe, Marines number one. You give me chop-chop." "Come on, G.I., me poor Vietnam girl. No have mama. Give me C ration, hey you!" "Hey, soldier man, give me Salem. U.S. number one. Give me candy, soldier man."

Overwhelmed by the seeming innocence of the local children, the Marines dug into their pockets. Out came four packs of C ration cigarettes, sticks of Juicy Fruit, cans of ham and lima beans (better known to the line company grunts as "ham and motherfuckers"). The kids fought one another to get their fair share of the booty.

Out through the dusty midday sunlight strode a mamma-san. In clipped, static bursts of Vietnamese she told the kids to retreat from the foreigners. Good Vietnamese children, the kids minded their elder, backing away from the throng of Marines gathered around the vehicles.

"Hey, Marines, you want some boom-boom? Got nice girls, heya! You got carton Salem? She love you long time, no shit."

Louisiana looked at me and said, "Welcome to Vietnam. Land of culture and enlightenment."

The Motor T sergeant piped up from the truck cab. "You men want to get the kind of clap over here that makes your pecker rot off," he yelled, "just go 'head on and get some of that. Now get your slick-talkin', heart-breakin' asses on this fucking truck. In case you boys ain't heard, there is a damn war going on out there."

The men remounted the trucks, and the convoy pulled back into the wheel ruts that sliced down the center of Highway One. We passed village after village and were surrounded by running, screaming, waving children. All the kids looked alike: tattered clothes, rubber-soled sandals or barefoot, dark straight hair, and hungry eyes. The eyes of the children would haunt me later in the war. Never satisfied, those dark brown spheres glared out of deep sockets pleading for the smallest nicety, the least generosity. This wasn't the children's war, but like every other war it seemed to impact the children most of all.

And their fathers, the able-bodied men of Vietnam, had all been conscripted into the ARVN, or the navy, or the air force. Many others had run from national service to join the ranks of the insurgent Communist forces known as the Viet Cong (VC).

As the Ontos and the lead truck rounded a small hill, I observed in the distance the control tower and outer defenses along an escarpment that protruded from the northern edge of the airstrip into the vast rice paddy region of Dai Loc. As we drew closer, the sun glinted off the barbed-wire double apron and the concertina wire that ran along the top of the obstruction. Sandbag bunkers with rooftops four layers thick came into view. Closer inspection revealed the muzzles of M-14 rifles and M-60 machine guns protruding over the fronts of the sandbag parapets. Marine riflemen in dirt-caked jungle fatigues and flak jackets waved at our little convoy. The front gate sentry raised the barricade and we entered our new home, An Hoa Combat Base, home of the 2/5. Suddenly the war seemed real and close.

The mission was to find Victor Charlie and destroy his ability to wage war against South Vietnam. I later learned that many of the South Vietnamese sympathized with Victor Charlie. National kinship was one reason, but failure to understand America's military's mission was a quandary to the average uneducated Vietnamese. I would also learn about the methodology of the North Vietnamese Army (NVA) and its cadre of political officers and terrorists. But our drama would be played out in the Arizona, a Marine nickname for the Dai Loc and Duc Duc provinces and their surrounding villages and quiltlike panoramas of interlocking rice paddies stretching northwest of An Hoa

Combat Base. The Arizona covered several hundred square miles.

One sensation, deep in the heart of each new Marine infantryman arriving at An Hoa, was that finally our war had come and we would get to be participants. We promised ourselves that we would kill the VC and NVA unswervingly and unmercifully.

CHAPTER THREE

Battalion Jungle School—Getting Ready for the Arizona

After arrival at An Hoa, we were assigned huts (called "hootches") with rifle platoons. My hootch was in a neat row of wood, one-story buildings, each approximately twenty feet wide by thirty feet long. A corrugated metal roof kept out sun and rain, and the top half of the hootch was screened to allow ventilation. One screen door opened on the company area, to the front of the hootches. Platoons and squads lined up in formation in this company area for patrol orders, debriefings, inspections, award presentations, and ass-chewings of the nonofficial variety.

I was assigned to Third Platoon, Hotel ("H") Company. The Marine rifle battalion is a simple animal in theory: four companies of three platoons each, each platoon composed of three rifle squads. Each of the four rifle companies also has a weapons platoon and a command group consisting of the company commander (a captain), an executive officer (a first lieutenant), and a ranking enlisted man (the first sergeant).

15

Platoon commanders are first or second lieutenants. The ranking enlisted man in the platoon is the platoon sergeant (usually a staff sergeant or gunnery sergeant).

Hotel Company was commanded by Captain J. J. Doherty, who was a second tour Marine officer, and he had a veteran's disdain for caution on the battlefield.

After three days of Battalion Jungle Warfare School, I had been issued a new set of loose-fitting jungle fatigues. The "jungles," as they were known in the bush, were very baggy and had large pockets on the thighs and both breasts. With their gaping pockets, jungles were good for stowing extra magazines, ammo, cigarettes, food, and, of course, piastres, the currency of South Vietnam. We traded in our Stateside leather combat boots for lightweight canvas-topped jungle boots with steel shank insoles (to deflect punji stakes).

All Marines in I Corps were issued flak jackets, sleeveless padded olive drab vests with interlocking fiberglass plates sewn into the front, sides, and back. These Kevlar panels did an effective job stopping shrapnel fragments from grenades and mines. This protection was much appreciated in the Arizona, which was a nightmare of booby traps, minefields, and explosive devices of every sort. In my battalion it was standing orders that the flak jacket be worn at all times by all personnel in the field.

The officers of the 2/5 all had their standard orders for the field, specifically: "Yea, though I walk through the Valley of the Shadow of Death, I will fear no evil because I am a United States Marine and the meanest son of a bitch in the valley." They added to that glorious attitude that all Marines shall wear their flak jackets no matter how uncomfortable, hot, humid, or clumsy.

The best, most revered, and most eagerly received piece of equipment issued to us was the "U.S. Rifle, Caliber 7.62mm M-14." This rifle was an improved and updated version of the venerable old M-1 rifle, which had made our country's enemies shudder across Pelilieu, Tarawa, Guadalcanal, Saipan, Tinian, and the bloody shores of Iwo Jima. The M-14 was an air-cooled, gas-operated, semiautomatic, shoulder-held, magazine-fed rifle with a selector switch to allow the choice between semiautomatic and automatic fire. The magazine was a detachable metal box that held twenty rounds of ball, tracer, or armor-piercing ammunition.

The M-14 with its Caliber .308 (7.62mm) NATO bullet shot ballistically, the same as the M-1 rifle with its higher powder capacity casing in Caliber .30 or .30-06 designation. Both rifles firing the standard military ball 150-grain bullet would push the projectile 2,800 feet per second at the muzzle. The M-1 with its greater case size Caliber .30 became U.S. standard in 1906, and its .30-06 bullet would perform better at ranges in excess of 1,000 meters or when pushing a heavier bullet. Accuracywise the marksman could take his pick. Although I had personally qualified expert on the U.S.M.C. 500-meter "A" course with both M-1 and the M-14, I shot a higher score by eleven points out of a possible 250 with the M-14, and did not miss the bull's-eye at the 200 meter standing, 200 meter sitting rapid fire, 300 meter sitting to kneeling slow fire, or the 300 meter, prone, rapid fire strings. I dropped points at 500 meter, slow fire, prone, although all my bullet strikes were bull's-eyes or in the four ring. The rifles I fired for qualification were not match weapons and yet every shot I fired was in the killing zone. The killing zone or mortal wound zone in rifle combat marksmanship is that area of the target representing the torso of an enemy soldier running from right armpit across the chest to left armpit and from the line across the collarbones down the torso to the solar plexus. This area would describe a circle approximately 12 inches from right to left, or across the chest and about 12 inches from the bottom of the throat to the bottom of the chest cavity. This 12-inch-diameter circle is the exact size of the bull's-eye on the standard U.S.M.C. "A" Target. A combat hit in this area on an enemy soldier will likely produce a kill, or at least a serious life-threatening wound in the chest area. Since the VC and NVA soldiers did not have the medical facilities or the helicopter-aided medevac capability that we had, a chest hit put an enemy trooper in very deep shit. Shooting to this center mass area of an enemy's body was Standard Operating Procedure, and later at First Division Sniper School, which I attended in March 1967 at Da Nang, that principle was made into a science.

I was now a jungle-fatigued, helmeted, jungle-booted, flak-vested, M-14 rifle–equipped member of the baddest-assed fraternity in the history of combat. I am not alone in admitting I was eager to stroll through the lovely (green and lovely like the Cobra) Arizona Valley and make the formal acquaintance of Charles, better known as Victor Charlie, our local Commie bad guy.

CHAPTER FOUR

Patrolling the An Hoa River Basin (Arizona)

From December 1966 through the first weeks of January 1967, the Marine rifle companies of the 2/5 had been sniped at and ambushed often while on routine patrols. The patrols were designed to project a physical presence in the many hamlets clustered around the north end of the An Hoa Combat Base. This physical presence was intended to convince the local peasants, their elders, and their leaders that a friendly force was attempting to neutralize the Viet Cong threat in the Duc Duc and Dai Loc provinces. Several Marine patrols were in the field daily. These patrols varied in size and mission. Squad-size patrols covered up to fifteen klicks (kilometers), or ten miles, on a daily routine show of force through villages and their rice fields. A squad-size patrol usually comprised not over ten Marines, including two extra Marines of an M-60 machine gun team that usually accompanied any patrol.

These patrols had been coming under pressure from the Viet Cong units in our sector. The main type of enemy activity was passive. The terrain of the region, rice paddies with trails winding around and through them, was ideal for concealing mines and booby traps. A favorite method utilized by our enemy involved the staking of an empty olive drab C ration can to one side of a paddy dike entrance or levy trail, the open end of the can facing across the trail, or footpath, which was usually no wider than three feet. A hand grenade, type M-26 preferably, would be placed in the open mouth of the can by clever Victor Charlie. When the grenade was stuck into the C ration can, the grenade's spoon would be held safe by the can's walls. Charles could then remove the grenade's safety pin without detonating the grenade. A monofilament wire or some other form of trip wire was then attached to the grenade's head and run taut across the trail to another stake or a bush, or was secured in an earthen berm and camouflaged.

If a point man carelessly stepped onto his eightieth-odd dike that day and one of his jungle boots tangled in fishing line he could not see through the rivulets of sweat streaming down his face, the tug on the line would pull the grenade from the can, the safety lever (spoon) would fly free (causing an audible *twing*) and the grenade's firing mechanism would ignite, giving the patrol about four seconds to get into the paddy's mucky water or suffer the consequences.

Far too many infantry personnel were lost to mines and booby traps in the Arizona Territory. Yet the mission of the 2/5 was to pacify the indigenous population of the Duc Duc and Dai Loc provinces. How could the battalion continue to mount and operate patrols but minimize casualties? The casualty rate in

Vietnam was very high, and the Marine High Command at Da Nang was concerned.

The commanding general (CG) spoke to the Marine First Division General Staff early in January 1967: "I want each of you officers to consider that our enemy is led by guerrilla officers that have as much as twenty years' experience fighting the Japanese, Chinese, and the French. They are too cautious to face our regiments in open combat. The Viet Minh cadre hope to wear us down and obtain political relief from the American citizen on the street. Just as Napoleon faced a doubting Paris in 1812, we also must seek a Waterloo-like remedy of sorts. We must entice the enemy to close with one of our best battalions in what appears to be a do-or-die situation. We will then attack the Communists and destroy them. Gentlemen, I leave the details of the match to your industrious planning. Just give me one day to turn Two-Five loose on that local main force battalion and their NVA advisers and I'll guarantee you, gentlemen, I'll put those sneaky bastards out of business forever. Please provide a plan using Two-Five as the assault element and ensure that the support is there to cover all contingencies. I will see you all back here at eighteen hundred hours sharp!"

The staff officers stood as one and acknowledged the commanding general of the First Marine Division: "Aye, aye, sir."

The assistant commander, who was himself a one-star general, added his observations regarding the CG's instructions: "General, I suggest we attempt to drive the enemy from his sanctuary in the Arizona

Territory specifically along the Song Thu Bon Valley in the vicinity of Phu Loi Island. We can employ three companies to sweep the enemy into the open paddy and by close pursuit force his concentration at a natural obstacle like a river ford or hillside valley. Utilizing one or two companies from Two-Five or One-Twenty-six, we can effectively block out any escape route and dispersion attempt. In this manner, we can close with Charlie and crush him between the sweep and blocking companies."

"Well, it sounds like a plan to me," the general responded. "But in the event Charlie hits a tunnel complex or friendly village and escapes, I will order Two-Five to assault directly into the main force battalion headquarters at Phu Loi. That way Charles will have his back to the wall and be forced to fight. Then it will be a bloody day. Either way, we get the Commies out of the way and get on schedule pacifying those villages. I want to try it the easy way first, using the blocking forces along the Song Thu Bon."

"The staff will get to work on the logistics immediately, General."

"Very well, I want troops in the field and on the march by week's end."

"The general can count that done, sir!"

CHAPTER FIVE

Company Sweep—
Duc Duc Province

The first week of January 1967 was occupied by frenetic patrolling of Arizona Territory by the Fifth Marine Regiment. The 2/5 had its rifle companies rotating patrols and manning perimeter security lines at An Hoa. Orders came for Hotel Company to saddle up for a day-long sweep through a series of villages in the rice basin of Duc Duc Province. To the northeast of An Hoa, Duc Duc encompassed the territory bordering the Thu Bon River. This was enemy territory. Every man took hand grenades and extra ammunition for his M-14 rifle. Some Marines were designated "lawmen" and carried a pair of M-72 LAWs, olive drab launchers containing antitank rockets that could blast through eleven inches of concrete or an earthen bunker. Each platoon had two two-man M-60 machine gun teams with a gunner who shouldered the M-60 and a loader who carried extra ammo. Other Marines on the mission also carried extra machine gun ammo in canvas-covered boxes containing one hundred rounds of belted 7.62mm ball ammunition.

In short, the company was loaded for bear. We even

had a team that humped a 60mm mortar, which was highly effective against fortified structures or against troops caught in the open. The ammo bearer grunts carried both high-explosive and white phosphorus mortar rounds on top of the ponchos strapped to the tops of their haversacks.

Each platoon formed up on the company street in front of its hootch. Platoon sergeants inspected each Marine's gear. Every man carried three or four canteens of water from the back of his web cartridge belt. After the inspection, the platoon sergeant faced about and saluted the platoon commander: "Sir, all men present and accounted for." At that point, the lieutenant in charge of the first platoon turned to the men and proclaimed, "Today the entire company will patrol Duc Duc along the river. Keep your eyes open for enemy positions at village entrances and in the tree lines across the paddies. Return fire only when fired upon. Any orders to fire at targets of choice will be given by myself or Gunnery Sergeant Gutierrez. Keep a ten-yard interval in the paddies and cry 'Fire in the hole' if any man triggers a grenade or mine. Listen to your squad leaders, and if the shit hits the fan, control your rate of fire on target. The company commander will have artillery support on the way if we get bogged down. Good luck, men. Saddle up and assume marching order. Third Platoon, take the point. Where's my radioman? Where is PFC Cross, dammit? Let's go kill some dinks!"

We filed out the dirt road leading across the perforated steel plates of the An Hoa airstrip and along bunkers manned by Echo Company. We marched across the double barbed-wire apron hung with empty tin cans and populated by claymore mines, then moved single file out into the surrounding rice fields.

The morning hours were spent crossing endless paddies, only to enter another half-deserted village of thatched huts housing mamma-sans and their small children. The mamma-sans smiled with hands cupped, begging for food or cigarettes, while the children mobbed us and tugged at our utility trouser legs. We gave the kids gum and candy while we had them, but there was never enough to go around. Looking at these simple people in their meager surroundings made each of us wonder what the hell we were doing over here in Vietnam instead of cruising back home with Sally and Linda. We searched the villages for weapons caches or rice supplies bundled and kept to pay as taxes to the Viet Cong and their NVA mentors. We trooped through each village's lone street and out into another expanse of rice field. The villages were like small dry islands in a giant sea of rice.

The entire company was strung out along a zigzag system of paddy dikes for a quarter of a mile. Each Marine minded his own business and concentrated on his footing in the muck and goo of the paddies. The going was painstakingly slow, and Hotel Company had a thousand meters to cover before reaching the safety of the far tree line and the next village's huts and walls. Just at that moment, the hot, fetid air was split by the *crack, crack, crack* of AK-47 assault rifles firing from our port (left) rear at seven o'clock. The Viet Cong had allowed us to pass their position until our rear flanks were exposed, because it was difficult for us to return fire from the head of the column across the main body of the company. Then the metallic crack of the AK-47s was joined by the duller thumping resonance of a heavy crew-served machine gun. Bullets cracked and sizzled through the air over our heads, and Marines who had been walking along the top of the dikes jumped prone into the paddies. The heavy machine gun continued its fire in short, methodical bursts. After a few moments the beaten zone was established by the VC gunners and their fire coned in on top of the prostrate Marines. Great chunks of earth were torn off the protective dike walls and pitched into the air by the heavy machine gun bullets.

I fell, not into the paddy water for safety, but crouched into a kneeling position on both knees, and shouldered my M-14 rifle. I could see the muzzle flashes of the machine gun about four hundred meters away, across the expanse of paddy to our left rear. I aimed my rifle in the general vicinity of the muzzle flashes and began to squeeze the trigger. My M-14 barked angrily as I fired round after round over the heads of our downed troops into the jungle at the edge of the rice field. I emptied the twenty-round magazine and was loading a second when Charlie Mexico yelled, "Get down, you crazy gringo, we got arty [artillery] on the way." But adrenaline was coursing through me so hot and strong that I barely heard. Then a pair of hands grabbed my flak jacket and jerked me into the safety of the paddy water. I shoved my helmet against the earthen wall of the dike and listened to the raging pulse of my heart as the first incoming artillery round smashed into the paddy in front of us. The explosion was humongous, and although I had heard many 105mm howitzers working the nightly harassment-and-interdiction fire missions at An Hoa, I knew that this artillery was much more powerful.

The captain was on the hook (radio), adjusting the artillery. Another round of artillery zoomed over our heads and erupted another two-hundred meters closer to the tree line. Gray smoke belched from the impacted shell crater. One of our machine guns coughed into action, pouring a stream of red tracer bullets into the tree line where the enemy machine gun's muzzle flashes had appeared.

The captain had the artillery add fifty meters and gave the order to fire for effect.

We were not prepared for the sound or the reality of four rounds of eight-inch, self-propelled howitzer shells screaming over our heads. It sounded like the vibrations of a giant locomotive's steel wheels, with a wailing scream followed by a shuddering impact and explosion that lifted an entire section of the jungle into the air. One round exploded after another, turning the area where Victor Charlie had been hiding into a tossed salad of broken and shredded bushes, vines, and trees. How could anyone live through that?

Word came down the line to get saddled up and back on the dike trail and move our butts into the village, just a klick distant at the edge of the paddy. We got to our feet and adjusted our gear, then started off slowly, gradually picking up the pace as the two hundred or so Marines of Hotel Company snaked like a huge centipede through the field. I sighed and felt we were secure. I reached into my utility jacket for a Camel. Suddenly, Charles opened up again with the AK-47s and the heavy machine gun, this time directly from our port flank. Bullets cracked and whistled over our heads and between our legs as we ran laughing and crying through the paddy into the protection of the village.

I fell into a heap of Marines just inside the earthen wall of the village, landing on top of John Lafley, from Montana. Lafley was long, thin, and tough and had experienced hard combat up on the DMZ. Next to Lafley was Luther Hamilton, a red-haired homeboy from Oklahoma. Charlie Mexico was trying to conceive of new expletives for Charles, and as the ranking Marine in terms of time in the bush, Mexico was entitled to hate Charles all he wanted.

"Ay, *chingada*, that son of a whore dog mother. Charles always finds a way to fuck with us. *Perro cabron* bastards. Someday, I'm gonna do some damage to his ass."

"All of us share that sentiment, Mexico. But how can we get out of this god-forsaken village?" shouted Lance Corporal John Matarazzi, the baddest dude in Nam with the M-60. Matarazzi was of Italian ancestry, from Pittsburgh, and had survived the DMZ along with Mexico, John Lafley, and Luther Hamilton.

Just then, when things were starting to loosen up, Mexico yelled, "Get down, boys, the captain has called in more artillery on Charles's ass. Get some, Captain, let's kill these Commie *mojados* and get our asses back home."

The moment Mexico finished his speech, the artillery boomed in the distance and a half dozen rounds of deadly eight-inch howitzer fire came arching down on the rice paddy world of Hotel Company, Second Battalion, Fifth Marines. The eight-inch rounds tore into the paddy, ripping the landscape upside down. Immediately, giant shards of shrapnel spun through the trees and thatched huts in the village.

Mexico was furious! "Dirty bastards, we moved our position since the last fire mission. This shit is right on top of us, you crazy *pendejo cabrones*. I only got sixty days left; I'm too short for this bullshit."

Despite the near miss, in a few moments down the lines came the order, "Saddle up, move out." We got to our feet and dusted ourselves off to begin the four-hour march back to An Hoa and a hot meal. I think it was at this time that I began to understand Charles more clearly. Charles never got to rotate Stateside and buy a new car, nor did he get to visit his many friends—the war had killed most of them. Charles was a career player, and the only way to put him out of business was to catch him outside the protection of his bunker or his tree line trenches and make him stand and fight. If we could just make Charles spend an afternoon playing the game our way, I was sure we could get his attention. Permanently!

The march back to An Hoa was long and tedious. It was always painstaking to cross large paddy fields in the Arizona because of the constant need to be aware of mines and booby traps. When we finally rounded the last bend in the trail that led up the protective escarpment to An Hoa, it looked like home, and the thought of a hot meal was more than appetizing to me. I was beginning to feel the longer-term strain of what would become combat fatigue for most of us who patrolled the Arizona day in and day out. When Hotel Company stood down to man lines, it was like Sunday in the park.

CHAPTER SIX

Patrol Along the River

The platoon sergeant called the First Squad of Third Platoon together in our hootch after morning chow.

"The captain has ordered me to take a reinforced squad into the Arizona along the river to scout out the villages for VC, weapons and ammo caches, and rice. I've chosen First Squad because you have the most time in the field. We're taking Matarazzi's gun team, and Private Ivey will bring a couple of M-72 LAWs with him. In the event we get hit hard, there will be a platoon of Sparrow Hawk troops ready to helilift into the Arizona to support or extract us. We will be highly visible and we want to make contact with Charlie. I want everyone to take a box of machine gun ammo and extra ammunition for his own rifle. We saddle up in thirty minutes and move out. That is all."

We got our gear on. Utilities and jungle boots, trousers bloused at our boot tops, flak jackets and helmets. Metal chains around our neck held our G.I. dog tags, which had critical information such as blood type in the event we were badly wounded. We strapped lightweight canvas haversacks over our flak jackets. The haversacks were a dull olive drab discolored by use. We packed them with extra rifle cartridges, cigarettes, food, and socks—in that order of importance. On the tops of the haversacks there were straps to secure an entrenching tool and a rubber-coated poncho rolled up like a blanket roll. At our sides we carried bayonets, hunting knives, machetes, or magazine pouches holding extra twenty-round magazines. Some Marines carried first aid pouches on the right side of their cartridge belt. The first aid pouch held one large battle dressing, the kind that was used to patch a bullet or shrapnel wound and arrest the bleeding. Most men carried two canteens of water on the rear of their web cartridge belt. The machine gunners (and the platoon sergeant) carried the "U.S Pistol, Caliber .45" in addition to the M-60. The platoon sergeant's duty was to manage the squad and direct fire-and-maneuver rather than to be a main participant in battle.

We moved out across the landing strip, along the bunkers on the perimeter of the north side of the base. We greeted buddies who were manning the morning guard section of the perimeter fortifications. They returned our greeting with the standard expletives.

Our column executed a column-right formation through the barbed-wire apron and crossed the short path leading to the jumble of paddies that quilted the Arizona rice valley.

We spent the first few hours of the patrol crossing an endless matrix of rice fields. Some paddies were clustered with villagers knee-deep in the mud while they planted shoots of rice from cloth bundles tied around their necks and draped across their breasts.

Driven by men and motivated by the crack of a long quirt, water buffaloes in leather harnesses trod slowly through the mud and water. A farmer's son often rode atop the buffalo, a prince amid the splendor of his family's ancestral fief. Private ownership of the village rice paddies gave each hamlet its income and provided for the welfare of the people. Those villages and the sense of safety and freedom of their habitants were the targets that the Viet Cong and North Vietnamese hoped to disturb and ultimately control in order to topple the government of South Vietnam. The Marines were fighting to protect the villagers' way of life as well as the infrastructure of the South Vietnamese government. Although most of us had heard or read about corruption in the higher circles of the South Vietnamese government and the Army of South Vietnam, we felt that the villagers were honest and decent people and that our efforts to support and protect them were not without merit.

We stopped the column along a small stream that flowed into the much larger Song Thu Bon. Spreading out along the riverbank in the noonday sun, we smoked cigarettes and ate our C rations in relative silence. Just as we finished our lunch, a half dozen young girls in colorful dresses ran along the path on the bank opposite our position. We had broken security by allowing civilians to penetrate our perimeter.

"Some of you men detain those girls!" the platoon sergeant shouted. At once, half of us jumped to our feet and grabbed our rifles, preparing to run across the shallow stream to detain the females. Our progress was cut short by PFC John Lafley, who yelled, "Don't sweat it, boys, I've got 'em covered."

PFC Lafley had raised his rifle to his shoulder and from a sitting position, without moving from his place along our side of the bank, was tracking the lead girl with the muzzle of his M-14 rifle. *Blam.* The lead girl was knocked off her feet into the brush at the stream's edge. Lafley's rifle coughed three more times.

"Now, you gals just stay down there and none of you will get hurt." Lafley's voice sounded tinny after the heavy percussion of the rifle blasts. Several Marines got to their feet and ran across the stream to the fallen girl and her prostrate friends.

"Well, I'll be damned. Sergeant, come look at this mess. All these here are carrying grenades in their headgear. That first one is hit in the arm. She ain't dead!"

"Burns, get me the CO at An Hoa. Pronto."

"Aye, aye, sir," rasped Private Burns, the radioman for the patrol.

"Hotel Six, Rebel Raider has contact with Vietnamese civilians. Possible VC carrying grenades. One civilian wounded, noncritical. Over."

After getting the location, the CO responded, "Rebel Raider, this is Hotel Six. We have medevac chopper en route. ETA is ten minutes. Show yellow smoke. Then continue patrol back to An Hoa with extreme caution. Hotel Six out."

A few minutes later, the blades of the Sikorsky caught the sun's rays as the big medevac chopper sliced over the stream and settled onto the opposite bank, where the frantic girls lay clustered around their wounded friend. A couple of the men carried the wounded girl into the waiting chopper's bay, where the crewman put her down in the rear. The other girls were lined up, then their hands were bound with plastic restraining cords. All the girls were packed into the chopper, which immediately lifted off and turned its nose upwind, heading low to the southwest over the low-lying rice fields toward An Hoa. We knew the girls would be interrogated about the canvas bag of grenades and fuses found on their persons. If the Vietnamese and Marine interrogation teams found them to be Viet Cong instead of scared villagers forced to smuggle for the Viet Cong, they would be turned over to the ARVN authorities.

Their fate wasn't my problem or concern. We had five klicks of dangerous paddy to cross to get back to An Hoa. Every Viet Cong guerrilla in the vicinity had heard about the incident or been alerted by the gunfire and helicopter by then, and we were likely to step into some shit on the way home unless we were very lucky.

John Lafley—I called him the Montana Cowboy— had a simple explanation when the platoon sergeant asked just what the hell had made him shoot the girl without provocation.

"Hell, Sarge, it was just like up on the DMZ last year. The bitches was walking way too fast and not talking or nothin'. Shit, I knew those gals was up to no good. When I popped that first one, I saw all them grenades come rollin' out of her hat. Why, hell, I think I ought to get a commendation for restrainin' myself from cappin' those other gals. Shit, I just had a hunch, that's all!"

"Well, son, you are lucky they were packin' some grenades or the captain would hang both our asses for bustin' a civilian, and a girl at that! Jeez Louise, Lafley, you scare me."

"Hell, Sarge, I'm just proud to be a U.S. Marine. When they beat the truth out of those whores, they'll probably give the plans of the Viet Cong's damn headquarters to the captain. Hell, I've been here almost six months and I hardly ever seen any of these damn people a man can turn his back on. Just kill 'em all, let God sort 'em out. That's my motto." John Lafley, who had balls as big as the ones on the bulls he bulldogged at his ranch in Montana, spit tobacco into the dirt at his feet, then wiped his mouth with the back of a tanned hand.

"Let's saddle up and get our butts back to An Hoa, Platoon Sergeant; I don't think we've got enough boys to camp out here tonight, and Charles will be huntin' us startin' about now."

"On that note, I agree with the Cowboy. Saddle up, and let's beat feet out of this hellhole. Lafley, take the point. Move out. Watch out for booby traps and mines."

After three muddy, fly-infested hours, the patrol climbed the escarpment, then gave the password to the sentry and entered the Marine lines at An Hoa. Relieved and tired, all the Marines retired to their hootches and cleaned their weapons. It seemed to all of us that Charlie was laying back, not making prolonged contact, purposefully awaiting his time to engage. We knew the Marines had to make some penetration of Charlie's base camps, forcing the VC to defend themselves and to stand and fight.

It was early January 1967, and among the colonels and generals at First Marine Division Headquarters at Da Nang, speculation had it that Charlie was gearing up for a battle. Eventually, Charlie would see a tempting opportunity to ambush a trapped, defenseless company. Charlie would take the bait, and the First Division Marines would close the trap and hand Charlie his head. The heavy betting said the event was right around the corner.

CHAPTER SEVEN

The Jungle Trail

Our next patrol came the following morning. Two-Five's command was pushing us hard into the Arizona to flush out Charlie and to generally obstruct Communist infiltration of, and interference with, the village hierarchy. We fielded a reinforced squad with a buck sergeant as squad leader. John Matarazzi brought his M-60 machine gun team, and Ivey and another Marine carried a half dozen M-72 LAWs between them. With the two fire teams of riflemen and our navy hospital corpsman, the patrol numbered fourteen.

We carried plenty of ammunition for ourselves and canvas ammo boxes for the M-60. We had read about the First Marine reconnaissance patrol that had been trapped for three days by regular North Vietnamese Army soldiers and had actually run out of ammunition defending a hilltop against a vastly superior enemy. None of us wanted to run out of bullets during a fire-fight. In the Marine Corps, your rifle was your life, and that included a steady diet of 150-grain, 7.62mm ball ammunition. We also tried never to stray outside the friendly reach of An Hoa's artillery battery of six 105mm howitzers, four 155mm howitzers, and two long-range, extremely accurate and deadly, eight-inch self-propelled howitzers. In the event that our patrol took us over ten miles from An Hoa, we'd be out of range of fire support from the M-110 eight-inch howitzer, which had a range of 16,800 meters. We still had the option of air support, and we could call a flight of four F-4 Phantom or A-4 Skyhawks from Da Nang Airbase. The standard artillery M-101 A-1, 105mm howitzers could support troops only out to 11,000 meters, or half a klick over seven miles. Many patrols often exceeded that seven-mile distance and had to rely on the longer arms in the Marine artillery or fire support inventory.

We saddled up and again crossed the familiar perforated steel plates (PSP) of the landing strip. Down the line of bunkers, which seemed to grow another layer of sandbags each time the base at An Hoa was mortared, our patrol straggled by each position in the perimeter. After the ritual exchange of greetings between warriors, we marched into the paddies with our weapons locked and loaded. We strung out our column with the squad leader in the middle followed by the radioman. Lafley took the point and cut the paddies into zigzag courses from tree line to village. The villages were the usual: sparsely populated with women, children, and men too old to fight on either side. The people smiled and begged for cigarettes and food. The kids ran up to us, hugging our legs and feeling the pockets of our jungle pants for candy, gum, or coins. We filled our canteens at the village water holes and always added a halozone (water purification) tablet to the filled canteen. Disease in Vietnam, as in any tropical country, was rife, and our officers sought to keep us healthy. A cut or puncture from jungle foliage, a slip, or a fall would be a pus-filled sore in hours. As well, most of the grunts had scars on their legs and arms called "Gook sores." These were caused by the hot weather coupled with the general unsanitary conditions and constant immersion of one's body in the quagmires of germ-ridden muck and filth called rice paddies.

Finally, we cut across a small rice paddy and into a tree line that led down a shallow hill into thicker jungle. The trail we followed meandered through increasingly thicker jungle growth that had not been manually cleared like most paddies. In jungle terrain, the squad had to close the interval between Marines in order to maintain contact between men so that the point man, at the head of the column, could pass information to the squad leader and weapons team in the event the enemy was sighted. The point man had the critical responsibility of deciding which trail to use for an approach to an objective such as a village or a hill. If the point man felt an ambush was imminent, or that the terrain features dictated extra caution, he would modify his speed or describe the problem back to the squad leader, who controlled the squad's movements. The point man was the eyes, ears, and brain of the squad leader anytime new terrain was negotiated.

The squad had not gone over a klick down the trail when an opening appeared to the left. Partially obscured by the brighter rays of sunlight filtering through the jungle canopy, which to that point had shadowed the trail, the opening was actually a junction. Three young Vietnamese men dressed as farmers, in black pajamalike pants and linen-colored loose-fitting smocks, strode onto our trail. They wore cloths bound around their heads and were clad in sandals. The three men appeared to be in their mid-twenties and carried only the walking sticks typical of village rice farmers.

The squad leader ordered the point man to halt the farmers for identification. As Lafley and I, the first two Marines in the column, approached with rifles ready, the farmers exchanged some hasty words, then abruptly turned their backs to us and began running back down the winding trail. I raised my rifle and fired a couple of quick snap shots at the back of the last man.

"Cease fire, cease fire," the squad leader roared. "Those are civilians and they are not armed. Culbertson, you and Hall chase them down. Do not fire unless fired upon."

"Aye, aye, sir!" PFC Hall and I chorused. I took the lead, with Hall at my shoulder, and we sprinted down the jungle trail, which was intermittently lit by breaks in the jungle canopy. We quickly caught sight of the three Vietnamese, only to lose them around the next bend in the trail. My lungs were afire as the three farmers came into clear view and cut off the trail to the right, onto a plowed potato patch. The Vietnamese had to hear the *clomp, clomp* of our jungle boots pounding onto the hard-packed trail right on their heels. The Vietnamese ran at a right angle to the trail, directly across a small plowed clearing, toward another blur of verdant green foliage at the potato patch's periphery.

With no warning whatever, the air exploded over our heads, and PFC Hall and I dived for the deck and cover. *Blam, blam, clack, clack, clack, clack* went an AK-47 inches over our heads. I threw my rifle into my shoulder and from a range of not more than thirty meters fired a volley into the running farmers. It seemed like minutes, but the encounter had lasted only a few seconds. The incoming gunfire lifted, and the three farmers were gone, disappearing into the jungle at the far end of the field.

The rest of the squad came running up to our position. Lafley yelled, "I saw dust fly off the back of that dude's shirt. You definitely hit him, man."

The squad leader, whom we called Sergeant Mac, gasped, "You broke up an ambush. Those assholes were Viet Cong, probably trying to lure us into that killing field, where their buddies with the AKs were waiting."

"Hey, Sarge, look over here by the jungle wall where these dinks escaped. Lots of bloodstains. I think you guys clipped all of those bastards. They won't go far without medical help."

"All you people listen up. I want you to spread out on the way back. These Viet Cong are no dummies, and they might loop back on us up ahead. We're stuck on this trail. Lafley, keep your eyes peeled, and if we see anything let's kill it."

"Culbertson, I'm logging this as three Cong 'wounded, probable.' My guess is they'll never make it through the night. Good work and good shooting.

However, in the future you will not cap any civilian unless so ordered. The rest of you men, remember: Never, never underestimate your enemy! Just because you don't see Charlie doesn't mean he's not around; you can bet your sweet ass he's out there and he can damn sure see us." Lafley had been in-country the longest, and without really understanding why, I knew he was right.

CHAPTER EIGHT

Patrol to Phu Loc 6

The patrol threaded its way through the myriad of ripe fields back to An Hoa. We entered the wire defenses and marched to our company area, to learn we would be running convoy security to Phu Loc 6 first thing in the morning. We cleaned our weapons, a procedure religiously followed in the Marine Corps. We were always to be prepared to defend and repel an attack on our base, and to accomplish that function each Marine had to shoulder a clean, fully operational weapon. Personal hygiene and chow could wait.

After our rifles and machine guns were field-stripped and cleaned in solvent tanks and meticulously oiled and dry-fired, we went to the showers. The dark mud from the endless trails and rice fields was washed, scraped, and scoured off our bodies in showers of tin and canvas. The water was two temperatures: cold and freezing. We brushed our long hair clean and swabbed our teeth until we returned to a reasonable semblance of human beings. Our utility uniforms were cleaned in An Hoa by local villagers allowed inside the base to collect our clothes as required. After donning clean jungle utilities we felt practically brand-new. After a hot meal, the troops all retired to their hootches for some smoking and card game fellowship. Mail was delivered to Marines who had just returned from the field, and most men used the time to reflect on better days back home in "The World." Lights were officially out by 2300 hours and all the troops not manning the defensive perimeter hit the sack.

The next day came early. All hands were at chow by 0630. Orders came down to the individual platoons by 0730. Third Platoon of Hotel Company was to accompany an engineer team's six-by trucks sweeping the six-plus miles of Highway One toward our firebase at Phu Loc 6.

Third Platoon saddled up and formed ranks in the company street for inspection by the platoon leader. We had just received our new platoon leader, First Lieutenant Smith. The ranking staff noncommissioned officer in the platoon, Gunnery Sergeant Gutierrez, was the man with the stroke of genius and leadership status in Third Platoon.

We wound our way through the bunkers and across the wire defenses into the paddies of Arizona Territory. We picked up Highway One running from An Hoa to Da Nang and fell into two columns behind the engineer truck. Sweeping operations would not begin until we got a klick or more into the field. Once we had covered a klick to the north, the road turned and wound to the northeast. The line troops fanned out fifty meters to each side of the roadbed, and the engineers walked slowly ahead of their truck, sweeping the road surface from side to side with magnetic metal detectors. For the next several hours, we slowly progressed up Highway One. The infantry on the flanks spread out, pointing rifles outboard to repel any ambush of the engineers or their vehicle.

Phu Loc 6 came into sight a half mile up the climbing road. The truck briefly shuddered as a fountain of dirt and mud burst from under the wheel wells. The explosion was deafening and was followed by a shock wave that knocked the helmets off troopers' heads. So powerful was the blast that the huge Marine truck was lifted like a toy and twisted, spinning in the air like a somersaulting acrobat. Clouds of dirt and smoke cloaked the carnage as the dying truck spun in its death throes. Small rocks and stones were shot into the air like bullets and covered the flanking Marines. For a moment, all the men stood looking at the detonation site. Then, slack-jawed, disbelieving, and unable to acknowledge the utter calamity that had befallen the platoon, the troops pushed themselves into action.

Stumbling over ourselves, Third Platoon faced outboard, forming a protective square to defend the downed engineers and their smashed vehicle. I ran toward the burning hulk of the truck and came across a wounded engineer. His body was so badly burned that he did not even resemble a Marine. Most of his outer jungle utility uniform was scorched, and his weapon and helmet were missing. I bent over him and stared for a moment into his blackened face and shocked eyes that gazed into space. His words were a tangle as he muttered, "Hey, man, can you help me find my arm? I mean, I just can't find my arm!" As I stared into his tortured face, he lifted a blackened, burned stump that had been his right arm up into my face. His glazed eyes pleaded with me, but I knew he was in deep shock and probably did not understand the implications of what had just transpired. I knelt and pulled his head against my chest, and just held him. Other Marines were screaming for corpsmen to treat the engineers caught by the explosion. Four Marines had been badly wounded and several others had slight cuts from the flying fragments of metal and rock.

I didn't move, and knew it was senseless to try to bandage the arm of my Marine. The broken bones of his arm protruded outside the skin along the forearm in several places. Suddenly, his body went slack in my arms, and I knew he was done. Lifting his face to mine, I gently closed his eyelids.

The lieutenant had already radioed the company commander at An Hoa, and a medevac helicopter was en route. We threw a yellow smoke grenade, and the Sikorsky H-34 slid into our loosely defended perimeter. Ground troops who had walked flanks for the now-destroyed engineer team carried wounded Marines into the chopper. The more serious were placed on stretchers and given plasma to sustain their blood pressure until they reached An Hoa. We zipped my dead Marine into a body bag thrown out of the chopper cargo bay by the crew chief, then hoisted his deadweight into the belly of the 34 and gave the pilot the thumbs-up. The chopper rose slowly, tilting its beak toward An Hoa and sanctuary for our fallen brothers. We all said a silent prayer that they would make it back to the hospital alive. Most of us hoped that the injured Marines would each have a million-dollar wound and get to go home after this unnerving incident. However, in the Marines, if you weren't killed or crippled, you would be back.

On the way to Phu Loc 6 I wondered what my Marine's name was. Nobody seemed to know or give it much thought, but I never forgot that final gasp of breath from his lips, or that haunted look in his eyes. I knew it could happen to me at any moment, and I promised myself to pay better attention and to not cut Charlie or his pals any slack that might get me killed.

CHAPTER NINE

Phu Loc 6, Gateway to Go Noi Island

Phu Loc 6 was actually a mechanically smoothed, bald knob no higher than two hundred feet. Around its crest Marine bunkers were cut into the sides of the hill in a 360-degree perimeter much like the lines at An Hoa, only in miniature. Barbed wire and explosive devices such as claymore mines were employed where enemy infiltration would most likely occur. The command post or bunker, along with a weapons pit for mortars, was in the center of the encampment. The officers and staff NCOs also had billets or dugouts to live in around the center of the top of the hill.

Commanders divided the lines into squad sectors, with each of the three squads of Third Platoon taking a crescent covering 120 degrees. My bunker with Lafley, Mexico, and Holloway was to the right of the road. We installed aiming stakes in front of our position to ensure that our outgoing fire would interlock with the fire from bunkers on our port and starboard flanks. Behind our fighting hole, we could call on both 81mm and 4.2-inch mortars for close fire support. We had M-60 machine guns in every third bunker, and many Marines had M-72 LAW tubes, M-79 grenade launchers, dozens of M-26 hand grenades, and tracer ammunition for machine guns and M-14 rifles. There were three full-auto M-14s per squad assigned to automatic riflemen. Tracer rounds were critical at night, because the naked eye could easily follow the flight and strike of the bullets. Once a platoon zeroed in on a nighttime enemy, the volume of fire impacting the targeted enemy personnel was devastating and impenetrable. Phu Loc 6 had never been overrun in the history of 2/5's tenancy. From the northeast quadrant of the hillside, the muddy Thu Bon River wound its ancient trail to the sea. The Song Thu Bon was a historic haven for Charlie and his allies.

We received word at around 2200 hours that night that Third Squad would do a visual reconnaissance of the land along the Thu Bon River. We were to take a machine gun team, LAWs rocket personnel, and a corpsman. The lieutenant came along to observe how we ran a search-and-destroy patrol in heavily contested enemy territory.

The patrol was scheduled to commence at 0630 hours. The route was fifteen klicks along the riverbank, then jogged off to the west into the lightly jungle-clad hills surrounding a half dozen villages of less than one hundred residents. Locally a lot of rice caches were known to have been prepared for Charlie. And the floors of the village huts also could have concealed bunkers where weapons or wounded troops could be hidden from the outside. Our task was to search for contraband weapons, rice, and personnel that sustained the enemy's ability to continue the war.

The night passed without incident, and we stood two-hour watches until dawn. By 0600 every Marine in Third Squad was saddled up with jungle utilities, flak vests, helmets, and very light haversacks containing extra ammunition and cigarettes. Some men drew extra hand grenades, which were hung by their spoons off cartridge belts. Each man took an extra hundred-round box of gun ammo. John Matarazzi and his assistant gunner walked over to our squad bunkers.

Matarazzi was a clean-cut, handsome, Italian, Catholic kid of nineteen. He was hardened from his tour with the 2/5 on the DMZ. Mat was probably the best machine gunner in the battalion, although his tightest buddy, PFC Gedzyk, also a veteran of the DMZ, would argue that point. We felt more confident when either Matarazzi or Gedzyk accompanied a patrol. Both gun teams were famous for getting their M-60s into action in a heartbeat. I had witnessed Mat running to the point of the platoon under withering fire to direct gunfire on Charlie seconds after the point was ambushed. The ability to set up the gun quickly and establish a deadly beaten zone was critical. Once the machine gunner had established fire superiority over the enemy soldiers, the rest of the squad or platoon could maneuver to outflank or cut off the escape route of the enemy. John Matarazzi was a skilled and deadly operator with his gun. The volume of fire of the M-60 machine gun would also penetrate all but the stoutest enemy fortifications. Common jungle foliage provided no cover whatever from an accurate burst of M-60 fire.

After a few canteen cups of Joe (coffee), we formed

up and checked our gear. Matarazzi always wore two bandoliers of machine gun ammo crossed over his flak jacket. Mat said he could feed the gun faster because the ammunition across his chest wasn't kinked. Personally, I felt it was the Pancho Villa profile that Mat imitated.

The Marines of Third Squad filed through the wire and down the road leading from the relative safety of Phu Loc 6 into the Arizona. The Song Thu Bon plodded along, a modest klick to the west. Lieutenant Smith treated me with undeserved courtesy. When we reached the first flat trail, he called out, "Culbertson, get on the point." There's a first time for everything, but walking point along the Song Thu Bon is a job for a veteran.

Inexperience aside, I had been on half a dozen patrols and participated in short, hot firefights with Charlie. Several of my brother Marines had been killed right next to me. I was one of the best marksmen in the company, if not the battalion. Since I was seven years old my father had taken me hunting in the wheat fields of Oklahoma. I had worn out the barrel of a Winchester Model 62 pump rifle before I was twelve. I thought I was definitely "point man" material, and with a bit of luck I'd make a damn good set of eyes and ears for the Old Man.

We had no rice paddies or dikes to cross, and I set a very fast pace along the riverbank. I clasped the pistol grip of my M-14 in anticipation each time we rounded a turn in the path. The far tree lines looked menacing, and I continually tried to spot safe cover we could use if we were hit. After an hour and a half, we encountered the first village and fanned out to search the huts.

The villagers watched us with blank stares. They knew exactly what the Marines wanted. Charles had been through that village like all the rest, but he wasn't at home that day. Charles preferred the nocturnal hours, when the Marines had no air support and it was much more difficult to employ and adjust artillery. The days belonged to the Marines, but the nighttime was Charlie's opportunity to move and deploy his forces.

A Marine started yelling, "Over here, I need some help over here." A fire team ran over to the straw-thatched hut the Marine had entered. Three men went in and the others kept their weapons pointed at the villagers who crowded around the violated hut. Inside, the Marine yelled, "Get out of there, you bastards!" Another man said in a commanding voice, "Check them closely for weapons." Then the reason for the commotion was revealed as three scantily clad Viet Cong soldiers were brought out into the village street. The Viet Cong were forced to squat with their butts resting on their heels. Their hands were securely tied behind their backs and their mouths were gagged with handkerchiefs.

Lieutenant Smith got on the radio and called the company commander back at battalion headquarters to requisition a helicopter to pick up the three Charlies and take them to An Hoa for interrogation. Vietnamese army interrogators would be waiting at An Hoa, and they would find out everything Charlie knew.

Soon a Sikorsky H-34 flew over the village and landed in an adjoining field. Lafley's fire team hustled the three VC prisoners into the chopper. The door gunner gave us the thumbs-up, and the big helicopter lifted off, turning its propeller into the headwind until sufficient speed was gained to bank southeast for the short hop to base camp. We were glad to get rid of Charlie; he wasn't our responsibility. Taking him along would only slow us down.

The lieutenant praised us, saying, "Good work, men. Every soldier or cache of rice that the Viet Cong lose makes their mission that much harder. If we hit their supply bases often enough, Charlie will lose the will and ability to fight. I am proud of each of you. Carry on!"

The platoon saddled up, and I reassumed the point, guiding the dispersed column onto the trail and out of the village. I kept the river to my left and walked fast along the straight stretches of road between the bends in the stream. Each time I approached a bend in the trail, I slowed down to look for trouble up ahead. The ability to sense trouble is a learned combat skill. Veterans tell the uninitiated that the sense improves in time until some troopers can feel the proverbial hairs on the back of their necks stand up when they come into harm's way. With practice, I got skilled at this combat intuition.

As Third Squad crossed some long paddies, I was especially careful to examine the dike entrances for booby traps. We did not stumble into trouble until we reached some solid footing on the trail to the next village. I first noticed a rough surface ahead in the trail. Upon closer examination the rough-textured area was a fifteen-feet-long by three-feet-wide oval in the dirt running away from the Marine column. If we had come under fire, we would have run across this area without much thought. Drawing up next to the beginning of the oval area, I knelt, and with my bayonet fixed to my rifle, I started probing the dirt. My bayonet slipped into the soil without resistance. Moving my bayonet from port to starboard across the width of the oval patch, I exposed loose fill dirt all through the area. After I probed the area for mines, charges, and wires, two Marines joined me and began lifting out the soft dirt. Eight inches down the Marines uncovered a loose layer of palm leaves on which the fill had been placed. The leaves were removed, and there was the trap—exposed and deadly. The pit was a good three feet deep, and the bottom held literally hundreds of sharp bamboo stakes. An errant step anywhere along the length of this punji pit would drive lethal stakes into the shin, thigh, or groin. If a man fell headlong, a stake could easily penetrate his torso. Deep penetrating wounds to the torso or chest were often fatal because punji stakes were frequently smeared with excrement, and in Vietnam's hot, moist climate the infections caused by the excrement could prove fatal.

I sidestepped the trap and led the squad off the shoulder of the trail and into the next village. We failed to turn up any Viet Cong or contraband rice or weapons. We also said little to the clustered villagers who begged for cigarettes. The older women stood out, with their betel-nut-stained teeth framed in blackened smiles. The younger women had the red-stained gums and teeth of the novice users.

The trail led through the village and across a dry pasture that had been left uncultivated. The fields and paddies in Vietnam, unlike most fields in the United States, were allowed to lie fallow and renew the nutrients in the soil after several crops were consecutively produced.

The terrain then began to rise drastically, and within thirty minutes we were climbing steep, jungle-covered hills that had no cleared trails or footpaths. Finally, I negotiated the ridge of a saddle that overlooked a large rice field that stretched toward a village about three hundred meters distant. I glanced to my left flank briefly as I fought off the elephant grass that cut the sleeves of my utility jacket and obscured my vision. To my surprise the paddy was dotted with men and animals. A quick count suggested upwards of twenty men and a half dozen animals plowing the field. The men wore farmers' black trousers and loose white shirts, but they appeared young and of sufficient age to be drafted—they should have been in the army of South Vietnam. The rest of our column had not yet come up to the ridge crest, where their silhouettes would be visible to someone below scanning the ridgeline.

I gave a flat-hand, palms-down motion several times quickly. The second man in the column stopped and knelt, passing the word that "point" had sighted something up ahead and wanted the squad halted and out of view. I called for a "gun up," and Mat hustled his M-60 to the top of the ridge overlooking what I believed to be enemy soldiers dressed as farmers. Mat positioned the M-60 on its bipod and ran a bandolier of belted ammo into the breach. Another hundred rounds was linked to the bandolier and laid out flat in the ammo bearer's hands so he could feed them to the gun. Four riflemen of the first fire team were placed alongside the machine gun by John Lafley, who silently pointed out the enemy troops to each man. No one spoke a word, and in fifteen seconds we had a machine gun team, a fire team of riflemen, and the point scout ready to open a volley of plunging fire directly into the target-rich rice paddy.

The lieutenant reached the crest and spoke out, as much in question as command, "Culbertson, what have you got down there?"

"Sir, I count about twenty dinks camouflaged as Luke the Gook farmers. They've got a half dozen water buffaloes, and no women or kids. It looks like a rice harvest for Charlie from here, sir. I recommend we open fire on these bastards before they get away from us, sir. There ain't one old geezer in the whole lot."

"Can you make out any weapons on any of those men down there?"

"No, sir. I don't think that they are armed. Lafley says that's how they run that phony farmer routine, so they don't get shot while they are bringing in a harvest, sir."

"Culbertson, Lafley, hustle down to the paddy and detain those farmers, or whatever the hell they are, and do not fire upon them unless they fire. I'm not going to get my butt jumped by the captain for killing some unarmed civilians. Matarazzi, you will hold your fire until directed otherwise."

Matarazzi chimed in, "Aye, aye, sir! But, Lieutenant, those assholes down there should be ARVN troopers at that age. I don't see any green utilities or uniforms. Those gooks are Viet Cong, sir, or that field ain't full of buffalo shit."

"Corporal Matarazzi, I understand your need to express your feelings for these people through the vibrant chatter of that M-60. However, no one can guarantee me what we've got. Culbertson and Lafley should be down to the paddy level by now."

"Holy shit, sir! Look at those bastards run. They're dropping plows and everything. Sir, request permission to pursue the enemy. Sir?"

"All right. Third Squad, go get those Viet Cong! Do not fire into the village unless fired upon!"

Third Squad tumbled down the thickly foliaged hillside onto a wide dike that ran parallel to the largest paddy. Smaller dikes ran away at right angles from the larger dike. Any zigzag route would take us into the first village at the periphery of the paddy system. It was to this first village that the VC fled after catching sight of our point men.

After negotiating the slippery mud and goo of the dikes and cutting across one shallow paddy to save time, we burst into the first hut in a long row of village dwellings. Only Vietnamese women and children were present. We yelled at them and mouthed the wide-palmed query, "VC, beaucoup VC, *di di mau*?" The women looked frantic, and all of them seemed to speak or cry out with shrieks and gestures: "VC *di di* Song Thu Bon! [The VC ran to the Thu Bon River!] VC number ten, Marines number one!" They pointed to every direction of the compass; their input was obviously no help. The VC in question were very likely their husbands, brothers, and sons.

Marine tempers flared! After shouted threats as to what would befall the people if they didn't get their stories straight, a Marine finally drew a K-bar out of his hip sheath. Grabbing a tall Vietnamese woman by her ponytail, the Marine practically lifted her off her feet and slammed her head against one of the main lodge poles in the center of the hut.

"Somebody tell this bitch I'll cut her fuckin' throat if she don't start making some sense. Tell her, dammit! I'm tired of constant bullshit from these assholes. Tell her."

At this point Lieutenant Smith flung himself into the hut and yelled, "Corporal, you will put down that knife. We are not here to kill women and children. Charlie is getting away clean as we speak. Corporal, that is a fucking order! Now, do it!"

Marvin Redeye was a full-blood Cheyenne, and all of that blood was pretty damn hostile. As he put it, "My people just don't jack around when we take the warpath, Culbertson. Hell, if we'd fucked around, Custer would have escaped. Know what I'm saying?" Redeye released the woman's hair and smashed her in the face with his fist. The woman dropped like a sack of rocks onto the packed dirt floor of the hut. "Fuck all these people, Lieutenant, I'm going outside for a smoke." No one said a thing.

Third Squad formed up on the street outside the hut. The lieutenant's speech was short and to the point: "Men, you caught Charlie cold today. Charlie escaped, and it was a chickenshit rule that cut him loose. We will have other opportunities. Be patient! I'm proud to serve with you men."

First Lieutenant Smith was obviously one good son of a bitch. The best officers were often second-tour captains and mustangs, officers who'd had prior enlisted experience. Smith seemed genuinely concerned with his men's welfare. Perhaps he would not jump at the first chance to earn a Navy Cross by getting all of us killed.

I later learned that decisions about "getting all of us killed" were rarely the province of first lieutenants; the Marine first lieutenant doesn't come into focus in the "big picture."

CHAPTER TEN

Arizona Territory, Communist Infiltration South

After we reached Phu Loc 6, Third Squad filed up the hillside and through the wire. It was 1930 hours and the sun was just setting. Flashes of crimson and gold sparkled on the meandering waters of the Song Thu Bon. It was hard for me to grasp that this lovely, peaceful ribbon of life that flowed so solemnly through the rice basins was also a highway of death. The Song Thu Bon supplied water to the richest rice fields in Asia. To tend the abundance in those fields, peasants lived together in dense village clusters. The plentiful rice brought the Viet Cong and his hungry North Vietnamese Army henchmen south to topple the free Vietnamese government.

The Marine Corps mission in the northernmost sector of South Vietnam was elementary. The Marines had to slow down the North Vietnamese infiltration into South Vietnam. The first method was pacification. Pacification presupposed that the local villagers and their hamlet leaders and elders would aid the

American drive to rid the countryside of the Viet Cong and the NVA. The fallacy in that mode of thought was that the NVA were so utterly ruthless that they would murder, torture, and destroy any elder, villager, or other local South Vietnamese who failed to cooperate with their plans to dominate the south. The North Vietnamese, with the overt aid of their Viet Cong allies, knew the dialect, customs, and traditions of the populace far better than the Marines and their South Vietnamese Army counterparts. The situation was frustrating for the leathernecks, who would have much preferred fighting a decisive battle to playing the multiple roles of politician, sociologist, and urban engineer.

Marine Command at Da Nang was pressing patrols into Arizona Territory to lure Charlie into a pitched fight. The Marine generals at Da Nang did not fear a match on Charlie's turf with his NVA advisers and regular troops.

In the aftermath of World War II, the Viet Minh leaders, later labeled Viet Cong, crushed Japan's last vestige of power in Cochin China, which had been dominated by the Japanese Imperial Army during the war. By 1946, the Viet Minh had fallen under the military leadership of General Vo Nguyen Giap, an infamous Communist leader. By 1954, the war of imperial conquest was forfeited by the French Army Airborne and French Foreign Legion battalions at the French river valley fortress of Dien Bien Phu. Again Giap headed a Vietnamese military staff that undermined the French high command.

The North Vietnamese army was now pouring men

and material into South Vietnam at a rate that the U.S. Marines were unable to halt—or even slow down. The Americans were unsuited to the jungle warfare waged by these guerrillas. The Vietnamese were clever and made shrewd use of the rice fields, jungle rivers, and hillsides. Whole armies of infantry, medics, supply porters, and their officers were slipping through Marine sweep patrols and blocking forces that turned up a few enemy soldiers now and then but usually allowed the main enemy body to escape.

The remedy was a pitched battle of sufficient scope to knock Charlie to his knees. Then the Marine brass would seize the initiative and through physical presence and intimidation turn the patchwork of hamlets in Arizona into safe havens for South Vietnamese political reintrenchment. The military backbone for the South Vietnamese government's pacification program would be provided by "Combined Action Platoons" composed of South Vietnamese militia soldiers reinforced by U.S. Marine infantry troops. The battle was coming, and every man on Phu Loc 6 felt the fight was too critical to wait much longer.

CHAPTER 11

Phu Loc 6, Waiting for Orders

Third Platoon perched high atop our hilly retreat. We gazed at the winding Song Thu Bon first thing in the morning and at dusk, before we split up into fire teams to guard the camp's perimeter. We ran patrols during the day into the Arizona through the string of villages along the river. We suffered a few short fire-fights in which Charlie pumped out a hundred rounds of small-arms fire at a patrol across a paddy and then scrambled for his escape tunnels before we could adjust and zero our return fires accurately.

Charlie had to have the terrain features and sun glare to his advantage. Charles loved to catch a Marine column rounding a jungle trail, facing into the sun, while coming up a rise with uneven footing and no ditch, trees, or paddy dikes to use for protective cover or concealment. Charlie would then fire AK-47s or SKS semiautomatic rifles directly into the point fire team. Marines rushing off the trail to escape the incoming volley would trigger prepositioned grenades and mines or fall into punji traps.

The last couple of nights on Phu Loc 6, a single Viet

67

Cong guerrilla had crawled to the base of our hill and fired several rounds with an SKS rifle at Marines exposed on the hillside. We nicknamed our new friend "Six O'clock Charlie." Actually, we felt sorry for Charlie, because in four nights of marksmanship practice, he had missed about everything on our hill. John Lafley had recruited three other Marines—PFC Burns, PFC Luther Hamilton, and PFC Paul Blocker—to march back and forth in front of the heavily sandbagged communications bunker, giving Six O'clock Charlie live targets to shoot at. As each bullet would *spang* off the deck at their feet or slap into the sandbags of the bunker, Lafley and company collapsed to their knees, laughing and pointing in the general direction of Charlie's last shot. I never knew if any of this humor was appreciated by old Six O'clock or not, but when Lieutenant Smith found out he nearly went ballistic.

"Are you shitting me, Lafley? You morons are trying to get yourselves killed over some fucking dink sniper who fires nothin' but Maggie's drawers [a white flag waved across a rifle range target when a Marine missed the whole kit and caboodle]."

"Sir, we were just tormenting that asshole. He couldn't hit a damn thing, really, sir!" Lafley tried to make light of the situation, but he knew he'd fouled up.

"PFC Lafley . . . or perhaps you like the sound of 'Private Lafley' better? You will disperse these Marines and never perform a feat of such blinding stupidity again. I do not want to write your parents saying their meathead son was shot in the head by an amateur Cong sniper while he marched in the open to show off his absolute lack of good sense. Get in your bunkers and stay there! That is all!"

All four members of the drill team sheepishly bowed their heads and intoned as one, "Aye, aye, sir."

The next night when Six O'clock Charlie showed up we were ready and waiting. After the first round whined off the bunker where we sat eating chow, Mexico and several other Marines stood up and fired a dozen rounds down the hill in Charles's general vicinity. Mexico and everyone listened in anticipation of another shot from Charlie, and when no gunfire was heard Mexico started jumping and screaming, "Got you, little *pendejo* bastard. *Adios,* Charlie, *penche cabron.*" Just as Mexico, the most experienced Marine in the platoon, uttered his last epithet, a bullet cracked by my ear and Mexico went down screaming.

"Jesus, I'm hit. That little son of a bitch shot me. Help me, man, get these fuckin' trousers off! I think I'm hit bad." Every man in the bunker was at Mexico's side by then. We held him still and unbuttoned his utility trousers and started to pull them off his hips.

"Doc, Doc! Somebody get the corpsman up. Mexico's been hit and it looks bad, man. Hurry!" PFC Lafley yelled up the hill in the general direction of the command bunker. The corpsman came running to our bunker carrying his olive drab medical bag over his shoulder. "Where's this man hit? I can't see anything until you men skin off his trousers, dammit!" The navy corpsman rolled Mexico onto his right side and, looking for a jagged tear in his side, exclaimed, "Good Lord, man, you're shot through the left buttock. There isn't even any blood. Somebody get him on his feet, and I'll get a medevac tag made out. That's PFC Charles Mexico, correct?"

"No, that's PFC Charlie Mexico, Defender of Liberty, Justice, and the American Way. Shot in the ass by old, sneaky Six O'clock Charlie for fuckin' around instead of minding his business." This insult was added by Paul Blocker, one of the Marines who had made up the original team shot at by Charlie. He didn't have much room to criticize Mexico.

"There's the chopper coming in from An Hoa, Mexico. Do you need some help getting up the hill? I think we got a stretcher around here somewhere," PFC Holloway quipped. Holloway was the luckiest man in the Fifth Marines. He could fall into a punji trap and come out with Charlie's wristwatch on. It was uncanny how a pint-size surfer from Southern California could survive everything Vietnam threw at him and come out smiling. Holloway always did, though.

Walking slowly, painfully, up the hill toward the chopper, Mexico turned in our general direction and yelled, "No way! Mexico don't need no fuckin' stretcher, you assholes. Mexico will return! You can bet your sweet butt on that." Just then a crew chief or corpsman in the chopper threw out an olive drab canvas stretcher and disembarked the chopper to help Mexico. With a renewed burst of energy, Mexico picked up the stretcher and flung it back into the chopper. "I said I didn't need no damn stretcher. It's bad enough I got shot in the ass. Man, this is disgusting; just get me the hell out of here!"

Every Marine present started waving. Several pulled down their utility trousers to expose their buttocks.

CHAPTER TWELVE

Blocking Forces Along the Song Thu Bon

Orders came from An Hoa the next morning. First Squad was to join the rest of First Platoon on Phu Loc 6 and await the rest of Hotel Company, which would be marching across Liberty Bridge in front of our position around 1400 hours. Third Platoon would then take the point and guide the rest of Hotel's Marines to positions along the western bank of the Song Thu Bon. The positions were to be dug in with a 180-degree field of visibility from upriver to downriver. The squads were to be divided into two fire teams, each team in one bunker, the bunkers approximately two hundred meters apart. Fields of fire were to interlock, and each squad would have one machine gun position and two automatic riflemen. Two 105mm howitzers had been helilifted to Phu Loc 6 with about one thousand rounds of ammunition. These guns would provide protective fire to shelter Hotel Company's positions and could fire preplotted fire missions into grid sectors along the river that were likely crossing points for the enemy.

Two reinforced rifle companies (Echo and Foxtrot)

were out sweeping the Arizona from a departure point some twelve miles to our east, across the Song Thu Bon. The companies, both from the 2/5 at An Hoa Combat Base, were linked up and running crossing patterns through the paddies, over jungle-cloaked hills and valleys, and through all the local villages. The companies' objective was to drive the enemy toward the river where Hotel Company was emplaced in carefully constructed bunkers invisible to Charlie from the opposite bank of the river. It was hoped that Charlie would attempt a night crossing at narrow points in the river. Then the blocking force Marines of Hotel Company would call an artillery fire mission from Phu Loc 6. The two 105mm howitzers would fire illumination rounds high over Hotel's position to illuminate the area of enemy activity. The burning orb of the illumination charge would fall suspended from a parachute, shining for around twenty seconds, before the flare would be immersed in the river.

If Charlie failed to elude the Marines of Echo and Foxtrot companies, the river was a natural barrier that the Viet Cong would have to negotiate to escape back into the myriad of protective hamlets in the An Hoa Basin.

Our squad ate a comfortable C ration meal and smoked a couple of cigarettes before we divided up the watches. I got the 0200-to-0400 watch, which I had expected as junior man. The 0200 watch, or graveyard shift, did not bother me. If Charlie came across our sector, 0300 to 0500 hours would be the ideal time to move. Troops on guard are generally tired and less alert just before dawn. But I didn't mind taking that watch, because I was certain not to miss anything! Maybe I would even get the first shot at sneaky Charlie as he lay motionless in a shallow-draft village pole boat.

The sun burned itself out over the river and seemed to melt into the dark silhouettes of the distant mountains. I lay back in my fighting hole, resting on the relative softness of my haversack covered by my poncho. My rifle rested against the parapet of my foxhole. My flak jacket and helmet were on the ground behind my head. Paul Blocker, salty veteran that he was, got the first watch—from 2000 to 2200 hours. Then Burns from 2200 to 2400 (midnight), and Corporal Kirby from 2400 to 0200 hours. I closed my eyes and focused on visions of Mom, Dad, and little Susie back home.

At exactly 0200, Kirby shook my shoulders and I was instantly with the program. Kirby was blond and stocky, and hailed from Knoxville, Tennessee. He whispered, "Culbertson, they're firing illumination about two thousand meters to our front. Echo or Foxtrot is pushing Charlie hard. If the activity gets within eyesight across the far bank, wake me up immediately. Got it?"

"Aye, aye, Corporal," I said as I slipped my flak jacket over my shoulders and fitted my helmet where I could just see the opposite bank of the river under the brim of the camo-cover. Night vision is hampered if you take in too wide a perspective or if too much light is allowed to enter your eyes. All I needed to worry about was my direct front. If Charlie came across, it would be smack in front of my position. I caressed the stock of my M-14 rifle, removed the magazine, and tested the pressure on the spring to make certain I had a full magazine. I was ready.

Behind me I heard one of the field guns at Phu Loc 6 report and send a round our way. *Pop!* The canister split high overhead, and a 20,000-candlepower illumination filament swung back and forth in an arc over the river. The opposite bank, the sand, and the water were as bright as in the daytime, and I feared that Charlie could see us and would not come.

I strained my eyes to the front, and sure enough, not two hundred meters from the bank the bushes were moving as men pushed ahead to the river. "Kirby, Kirby, wake up. The gooks are right in front of us. Wake up, man." Seconds later Kirby was awake and at the front of the bunker, scanning the riverbank. "Yeah, I got 'em now—they're coming straight toward us. Get Blocker and Burns up into firing positions."

The other two woke easily and grabbed their vests and helmets. The fire team got on line, with each man responsible for a field of fire to his direct front. Kirby spoke first: "Let them get in their boats and into midstream before we engage. I will fire first and you men open up at will. Is that clear?" We all nodded. We looked up and down the far bank, awaiting the first sign of Charlie.

"I got one. There he is, holding something at the water's edge about a hundred and fifty meters north of Culbertson. You pick him up yet? There are three more getting into a shallow boat. That first dink is holding a rope to steady the craft until his buddies can hunker down inside. Oh, shit, man—there's at least

ten more getting into boats all along that little cove."
Paul Blocker had great eyes and continued to give us
the play-by-play.

Several explosions flared five hundred meters to our
front. It appeared that Echo or Foxtrot was closing in
for the kill.

"Culbertson, what do you make those explosions
out to be?" Kirby was testing my ability to identify
weapon systems at night. It was important to know
what weapons were used by Charlie, because there
were specific ways of protecting yourself from different types of attack. A Marine did not react the
same to an attack by machine gun fire as he did to
mortar fire.

"Corporal Kirby, those explosions sound like M-79
grenade shells impacting."

"Good guess. That's exactly what they are, and
Echo and Foxtrot are close enough to spit on those
dinks." Corporal Kirby offered that last bit of information to underline the reality that Echo or Foxtrot could
get to Charlie before Charlie got free into the river and
into our rifle sights. The only thing I knew was that
this was one exciting happening! The sweat was running down off my brow, and my grip was slippery on
the M-14.

Burns hissed, "They're into the boats and pushing
off from the banks. I count four boats and about a
dozen VC. Man alive, Kirby, let's barbecue these
guys."

"Hey, Burns, you think the next bunker can see
these dinks from over there? I mean, if no one but us
can see these guys, then they're ours." Kirby and

Burns were buddies. Kirby had been raised in the southern Appalachian woodland; Burns was from New York City and profiled the hostile attitude of the city's mean streets. Kirby and Burns were naturals in Vietnam. Their survival skills were not in the least obsolete in that jungle hellhole.

"Lookee here, they comin' down right purdy now. Boats all lined up real nice." Kirby's excitement was felt by all of us. "PFC Burns, you got the honor of first shot. The team can fire at will after Burns opens up. Steady now, boys. Watch your sights and markers close!"

Burns's muzzle tracked the bow of the lead boat as it swung into midchannel and picked up speed. The reports of our rifles echoed off the far riverbank. Now the fire team was working over the Viet Cong boats. We were covering each craft from bow to stern with accurate and deadly plunging fire. The cones of rifle fire impacted with the boats and the surrounding water, and lifted the river's channel into a deadly froth. The heavy .30-caliber bullets slammed through men and wood as the boats were cut into kindling. Not a shot was returned from Charlie, so suddenly had the bullets poured into the fragile craft.

The rounds slammed into the wreckage of the Viet Cong soldiers and their boats. Bullets skidded off the fractured lumber that littered the water, and made a *whaang*ing sound as they ricocheted into the far riverbank. It was over in two minutes, and the last minute probably constituted overkill. Charlie was gone, somewhere under the murky water. Corpses and severed body parts turned up downriver later in the morning, but that was not our concern. As the old-time Marines in Vietnam liked to say, "Our business is killing Charlie, and right now business is real good!"

"Well, how about them apples, boys?" Kirby was pleased with himself. "They never even got off a shot! Hell, I'm sure we got all of 'em. Aren't you sure we got all of 'em, Burns?"

"Yeah, my corporal," replied the usually silent, brooding PFC Burns. "I think we tore Charlie a new one, although the skipper [the Captain] will probably ask why we ain't got no prisoners!"

Everyone laughed at the mention of prisoners. Burns was funny for a fat, freckled Yankee. Burns, like other Marines who had been in Vietnam for any length of time, could turn mean when the subject of killing came up. "Culbertson ain't a cherry no more! Shit, boy, you might just make a trooper with old Private Burns to school your ass."

I had passed the first test (the test of blood) in being accepted by this strange breed of fighter. A warrior breed who could joke and swear at you, and even defame your mother, yet in the next moment salute the flag from ramrod-straight attention, eyes welling with tears as the National Anthem or the Marine Corps Hymn blared from the golden throat of a trumpet.

Kirby and the other Marines in his fire team knew that Charlie would discover what had befallen his comrades by morning. The Viet Cong did not like to shoot it out with Marine patrols.

Now I was clear on the deserved reputation of Marine riflemen. Four of us, in less than sixty seconds, had killed a dozen men over a hundred meters away and cut their boats into kindling, leaving less wreckage than if they had been attacked by great white sharks.

CHAPTER THIRTEEN

Mortar Attack—North Blocking Force Terror

While Corporal Kirby's fire team of Blocker, Burns, and Culbertson was "firing up" the boat riders drifting down the Song Thu Bon, Luther Hamilton's fire team, far to the north, saw nothing. Luther Hamilton was a PFC from Bartlesville, Oklahoma. At 5'9", with reddish hair atop a mischievous face, given to constant high jinks, Luther was a derring-do, wild-assed teenager who was deceptively boyish looking and clean-cut. But the all-American image stopped at his looks. Luther Hamilton had a knack for finding danger and death, like other kids just out of high school. Luther had enlisted for two years in the Marines. In Recruit Training and Infantry Training Regiment, the Marines turned the Luther Hamiltons of America into "baby-faced killers" who set standards in bravery, aggressiveness, and total disregard for their own safety on the battlefield.

Luther manned his fighting hole, about one thousand meters north of Kirby's position along the same riverbank. Charlie did not seem to be penetrating the brush to PFC Hamilton's front. PFC Cross was with

Luther in the bunker and had a PRC-10 radio next to him with the handset attached to his helmet for quick transmission. The only problem with Cross was that he was "too short to climb out of the bunker." This being "too short" referred to the time remaining in a Marine's thirteen-month tour. In Cross's case, the time left in his tour was not much more than a week. We all knew dudes who got zapped when they were "new guys" in the bush, and careless, or when they were very "short" and got too cautious and uptight.

Manuel Ybarra was in Luther's team with a Corporal Lewis, a transfer from First Battalion, Twenty-sixth Marines. Ybarra carried his pack over hill and dale like a 200-pound six-footer even though he was more like 5'6" and 140 pounds dripping wet. Because of difficulty in clearly pronouncing his Spanish surname, all the troops called Ybarra "Yogi" (as in "Yogi the Bear").

Luther's team scanned the river on 50 percent alert. Half the team watched the bank for Charlie to sneak into view, while Cross and Lewis slept. Luther's hole was exposed to attack from the north and, unlike the other positions, was not protected on its flanks. When fireworks started in Kirby's sector, a second squad of Viet Cong was pushing its shallow-draft boats into the river half a klick upstream from Hamilton's position.

Charlie's boats drifted to midstream as Burns fired the lead round into his first boat. Luther Hamilton's team instantly came awake, all eyes straining toward our position as Luther's team sought out the reason for the very high volume of fire from the friendly side of the riverbank.

The second group of enemy boats slowly launched under Hamilton's fighting hole. The Viet Cong boatmen pushed long bamboo steering poles deep into the river. As the faces of Hamilton's squad, staring in our direction, were exposed above the bank, the Viet Cong opened fire with rifles and hurled Chi-com grenades over the riverbank. The fire forced the Marines down into their hole just as three grenades bounced into the bunker and exploded.

Wham, wham, wham, the grenades flashed inside the dugout, gouging out the earth as they exploded. Shrapnel not hindered by the protective red clay around the bunker's parapet sought out the huddled men, and burning-hot shards of casing pierced the Marines who sought cover against the front earthen wall of the shallow pit. PFC Cross took the brunt of the charge with his body and helmet. The protective panels of his vest did not let the shrapnel penetrate Cross's tender flesh. The steel helmet and strong plastic liner easily defeated the *spang*s of iron that collided with them. Unfortunately, Cross's face was exposed to the incoming steel. A large chunk impacted into his jaw and cut away the lower side of his face, knocking him senseless to the dirt floor of the bunker. All the other troops were wounded by the secondary wave of the shrapnel, but compared to Cross's wounds, their cuts and gouges were inconsequential. When a Marine gets hit, his comrades try to stop the bleeding, then treat the injured man for shock. No corpsman was available to aid the Marines in

Luther Hamilton's position that night. Just a bunch of scared kids.

"God above, turn him over, I can't see his face!" Hamilton yelled at a Marine down on one knee and staring into Cross's mangled face. "Jesus, where is the hospital corpsman when you need him? Shit!"

"Hey, Luther, I got a couple of battle dressings! But I can't see his face good, man," Manuel Ybarra mumbled from the center of the team. "Cross, Cross, man, can you hear me? He looks bad, Luther."

Corporal Lewis stammered, "Somebody get on the fucking radio. Man, Cross is bad. He needs to chopper the hell out of this shit, man."

"The frickin' handset was on his helmet, and it's busted!"

Luther looked into Cross's glazed eyes. The battle dressing they'd applied to his jaw was already leaking blood through the back of the bandage. "I'm going for help," was all Luther Hamilton said.

"What you say? Shit, Luther, this is nighttime. Charlie owns this son of a bitch at night—you know that, Luther. Boy, you're crazy as hell," said Ybarra, who had seen a whole team of Force Reconnaissance Marines ambushed up on the DMZ at night. After the Marines had been cut down, the North Vietnamese had tied their arms behind their backs and put poles through their arms. The Marines had then been carved up; their tongues were cut out and their privates were sliced cleanly off. Nobody wanted to see Luther Hamilton throw his life away. Hell, it was seven miles or more across silent paddies and up jungle-covered hillsides to get back to Phu Loc 6. Charlie would be moving out there under the cloak of darkness.

"This is bullshit, Luther. You got to stay and run the team," someone pleaded, searching for a bit of sanity in a tense moment.

"I'm going, and that's it! Cross is my friend. Shit, he don't have a week left in Nam, man! It ain't right! I'm going. Lewis, give me your .45! I'll be light that way. I'm running all the way to Phu Loc 6. Won't do no good to go to An Hoa, 'cause they can't help Cross in time, he's too messed up. Keep those pressure bandages on his face and elevate his head. I'm history!" Luther Hamilton slipped out of his flak jacket and put on Corporal Lewis's web belt with the .45 pistol and holster. "See you guys as soon as I can get back. Take care of Cross!"

Up over the parapet of the bunker, Luther's jungle boots kicked earth back toward his team. His form melted down the river trail to the south, and he blended into the night. "For God's sake, Cross hasn't come to yet! Somebody get his flak jacket open and listen to his chest. Is he breathing?" Corporal Lewis pleaded from the bottom of the fighting hole, next to PFC "Short Timer" Cross's prostrate body.

CHAPTER FOURTEEN

Luther Hamilton's Run to Phu Loc 6

Luther ran south from the bunker, along the river. After a hundred yards or more, Hamilton cut to the west along a minor trail that led across the southern edge of a giant rice field and into a sleeping village. Luther did not enter the hamlet, but jogged along the rear of the huts, keeping a close eye on the hootches for any sign of movement. Not a mamma-san or child could be heard. Not a single plaintive cry or bark from a dog.

At the end of a row of huts, another paddy matrix loomed in the distance. The murky waters of the rice fields shimmered. As he moved, the quarter moon would tuck itself behind the clouds, then momentarily reappear.

Luther knew a running man was easily observed. The hunter's eye picked up movement first, then calculated the configuration of man or animal that had crossed his vision. Luther sought tree lines and dikes to conceal his movements, but they were infrequent and more often he found himself on an expanse of road or paddy that was void of any concealing trees, bushes, natural berms, or rises.

Across the small paddies and expanses Luther would run, at a metered gait he thought would confuse an observer. His rhythm was very smooth to avoid drawing attention. The large fields and paddies required a more tactical assortment of movements. Luther crouched when walking behind short dike walls and crawled next to built-up trails, keeping low in the drainage ditches that straddled most roads. To cross the large paddies he employed a combination of crouched duckwalking, crawling, and measured walking between obscuring dikes, huts, and tree lines.

A tense group of Marines knelt over Cross's body back in the bunker, along the northern sector of positions blocking the Song Thu Bon. Visions of mowing Charlie down as he crossed the river had been abandoned for the time being. Everyone's attention was riveted on the lone Marine clinging to life on the earthen floor of the hole.

"Aaargh, aargh." Cross coughed to life and disgorged a torrent of blood and saliva that spattered the faces of his comrades as they looked on in horror.

"Get that dressing off the man's face! He'll choke to death." Corporal Lewis was the old man of the team and dispensed a fatherly compassion, albeit on Marine terms.

"Jesus, Lewis, Cross has bought it, man! I can't stop the blood. That chunk of shrapnel is embedded inside his mouth and probably has cut into his neck. Nothin' we can do now, man," Manuel Ybarra said.

"They won't run a medevac in here at night for one man, because it would spook Charlie and blow this operation. That don't do Cross much damn good, does it, Lewis?" Ybarra was frustrated and took out his hostility on the general condition of the war—FUBAR they called it, "fucked up beyond all recognition."

Cross sputtered and emitted a low, shallow moan, then grew suddenly silent. "That's it! That's fucking it for me, man! No more good guys from America helping the Vietnamese out of their stinking Commie mess. No way! From now on I'm cappin' these pygmy bastards and Hamilton can tag 'em and bag 'em. Cross was a good dude, man! He'd paid his dues in this shithole. Seven days left, and a man gotta die choking on his own blood in a nowhere, sorry-assed place like this. The gooks that threw those grenades in here didn't even know where we were at, man! Those bastards got lucky and killed Cross! He just wanted to go home." Ybarra had seen too much combat and needed a rest himself.

The combat cycle in Vietnam always repeated itself through changes in every infantry pogue in the Marines. First a boy came to a line outfit in Nam all charged up to protect the Vietnamese and kill the evil Communists. Then the boy saw some action and embraced the more practical considerations, like staying alive instead of living in an idealistic fervor for God and country. After the maturing Marine had seen some of his buddies killed and maybe been wounded himself, he became careful. Finally, he witnessed a situation of such unbearable sadness (like PFC Cross's death) that his only refuge from sorrow was anger. This anger fueled many a Marine's hostility toward Charles. In many ways, the cultivation of a high level of operational, tactical anger was necessary to forge a really deadly military machine.

Another row of huts came into view, as Luther rounded a bush-covered hillock. He held his breath! Just over a quarter mile off, as best as he could guess, lay the outlines of a row of Marine sandbag bunkers. Phu Loc 6 at last!

He made no sound as he reached the rear of the huts and crept into the open field behind the village. In his haste, Luther turned several times and lurched onto the dike leading away from the village. Slivers of moonlight played off Hamilton's face and arms as he turned into the rice fields.

Suddenly, angry shouts came from the periphery of the last hut, and Luther heard the high-pitched, clipped singsong of Vietnamese dialect directed at his fleeing shadow.

"Dong lai, dong lai," came the command to halt from the pursuers. Luther experienced an adrenaline rush and picked up speed down the dike trail.

"Marine, Marine, you die tonight," came the next nasal threat from the small group of Viet Cong guerrillas who had tucked in behind Luther's wake. The road was hard and dry as Hamilton sped along, clipping for the wire at Phu Loc 6, not four hundred meters away. His heart was pounding.

Green tracer bullets from Charlie's Chi-com assault rifles passed over Luther's head and ricocheted off the dirt at his feet. Hamilton picked up the pace. *Blam,*

blam, blam, clack, clack! Charlie was really working Luther over now.

Luther jinked off the trail onto the main road to the entrance to Phu Loc 6. Only 150 meters to go! A burst of full automatic fire sizzled over Luther's head. Turning while keeping his legs churning toward the Marine lines, Luther noticed red lines cutting into the night air toward Charlie. Yes! The Marines had picked up Luther's pursuers and had opened up with an M-60, firing a wide band of tracers over Hamilton's straining body. Charlie had turned around when the Marine machine gun bullets impacted in a beaten zone across the road.

Luther didn't stop running for a beat, but he turned his head and yelled, "Missed me this time, you Commie dogs." He high-stepped through the wire and into the arms of a Marine sentry.

"Where the hell you come from, man? You almost got your butt blowed away, but some dude yelled you was a Marine! I don't know who the hell this Marine is. Get on the horn to Company and tell the lieutenant or the captain we got a man come into Corporal Jones's bunker at oh five thirty hours. He got no helmet, vest, rifle, nothing! Charlie chased his ass all the way from the far village through the paddies to here," Corporal Stan Jones said, giving the rundown to his radio operator.

Hamilton got on the radio and identified himself.

The Golf Company gunnery sergeant said, "Hamilton, stand by, we already have a radio message two hours old from your company. One of your men crawled all the way down the trail to another hole to radio in to Battalion. Your man died five minutes after you left, but the CO wants to thank you personally after the navy corpsman has checked you out. Good effort, Hamilton, we can use more Marines like you."

After getting bandaged for lacerations to his knees and elbows from crawling over two miles along paddy dikes, Luther Hamilton caught the morning supply chopper back to An Hoa. Luther reported directly to the Battalion Headquarters of Lieutenant Colonel W. C. Airheart, Commanding Officer, Second Battalion, Fifth Marine Regiment, First Marine Division.

"Well, Hamilton," Airheart said, "I won't keep you, as I can imagine you are pretty tired. I commend you for showing leadership when one of your squad members was wounded. Company headquarters will put in a requisition for the Bronze Star. That is a very high honor in the Marines. If we were in the army, I imagine this act of bravery would be worth the Silver Star at least. However, we are Marines and we hold ourselves to a higher standard. That's why you joined the Marines, isn't it, Hamilton? To be with the best!

"Your CO, Captain Doherty, is, in my opinion, one of the most experienced, most able officers in the Corps. He will be taking your company and a sister company into the Arizona next week. We are going to catch Charlie in his home base and bring him to us, very close. We are going to squeeze the blood out of Charlie, Corporal Hamilton. But Marines are going to die, just as they always do in a battle like this one. I want you to tell your squad to worry more about killing Charlie and his NVA advisers, and worry less about your friends who get hit. Is that clear? Son, we will have extra corpsmen along and medevac choppers on standby for this match. Lance Corporal Hamilton, you did a brave thing today. I just want you to promise me that next week you will stick around and kill Charlie. I will take care of the wounded.

"See there, Hamilton, nothing to fret over! Get your men ready to go. This is the big one! That is all."

Luther Hamilton stood looking like hell warmed over and managed a textbook salute. "Aye, aye, Colonel. Sir, the men are ready to go. No problem about that, sir." Hamilton executed an about-face and dejectedly walked back to his hootch; Cross had been dead the whole time.

When the company got back the next day, everyone in Hotel Company wanted a word with the new hero. Rumor had it that Luther Hamilton had run seven miles, all the while pursued and fired upon by a platoon of Viet Cong, and had survived without a scratch.

CHAPTER FIFTEEN

Night Patrol into the Que Son Mountains— The Mission

By 1200 hours the remainder of Hotel Company had crossed the paddies fronting the main entrance to An Hoa, the same fields that only eight hours earlier Luther Hamilton had crossed to get help for PFC Cross. Cross came back to An Hoa, but he didn't arrive with the rest of the grunts of Hotel Company. His disfigured, bloodless corpse had been tagged and bagged and flown alone in a Sikorsky H-34 helicopter to the U.S. Naval Hospital at An Hoa. PFC Cross's body would be flown to Da Nang and embalmed and placed in a metal casket for transit to CONUS (Continental United States).

As the troops filed through the barbed-wire obstacles protecting the sandbagged gun emplacements of the perimeter defenses, opinions were exchanged.

"Man, I never saw nothin' like that before. Charlie must have lost his mind to cross the river like that," offered Lance Corporal Rivera, who had been around long enough to know how Charlie operated. "It was stupid, man. Charlie knew we had fired illumination all night. I'll bet we got at least twenty of them. Hey, you hear about Cross and Hamilton?"

"Cross bought it, man. He was a righteous dude, too. Everybody liked him," Gary Woodruff said. "He only had a week to do. Man, he was so fuckin' short he couldn't see out of that bunker. They killed Cross for nothin', and Hamilton ran all the way to An Hoa for nothin'. Hamilton ought to get the Navy Cross, man! Has he got a pair of balls on him or what?"

Recapitulation of the night's events continued up the escarpment, across the airstrip, and into the Hotel Company area. The exhausted Marines had barely slept, and they stumbled into the plywood hootches like zombies. Weapons were stacked by cots, and uniforms were discarded in heaps on the floor in each trooper's personal area. The heroes of Hotel's blocking force cast themselves into the sack, covered only by light olive drab blankets. In ten minutes every gyrene was off to dreamland; many were in nightmare land. It was a reality that eighteen-, nineteen-, and twenty-year-old men had great difficulty sorting out the truth and the reasons for the horrors to which they were constantly subjected. This problem, now formally known as post-traumatic stress syndrome, would bedevil many of the youngsters for the rest of their lives. That is, if they lived through the war to have a life!

By midafternoon, hunger had driven most of Hotel's motley crew to the showers and into clean utilities in order to properly present themselves at the battalion mess hall for a hot early dinner. The mess crew at battalion "busted their hump" to prepare quality chow, and plenty of it, for the troopers. In the Marine Corps there is seldom a restriction on how much a man can eat, providing he eats all he takes. *Nothing* was left on the stainless steel trays in front of the chowhounds of Hotel Company at that meal.

Back at the company area, the stuffed, still-sleepy men were delivered the bad news. Company Gunnery Sergeant Gutierrez, a short, stocky Mexican-American of thirty-five, addressed his flock.

"Men," he said, "the captain needs a sweep of the Que Son Mountains before we kick off the big operation that all of you know is going to clear Charlie out of the Arizona. Captain Doherty wants a reinforced squad with guns to run a ten-klick route through three or four villages in the mountains to our south.

"We got little sack time last night. But we gotta do what we gotta do. Hamilton will take his First Squad, Matarazzi, and his M-60 machine gun team out the south gate to the base past the dispensary and up into the hills. There are six checkpoints on the route. The commanding officer will coordinate the route with fire support. The artillery section will be firing H and I [harassment-and-interdiction] fire to stop Viet Cong night movement at chosen road junctions and on likely avenues of travel. Luther, your squad has to hit those checkpoints, then radio your sitrep [situation report] to the commander or officer on duty at company headquarters, An Hoa."

"Gunny, I'm fully rested, but my squad saw some pretty rough action last night. Nobody got two hours' sleep!" Hamilton said, not as an excuse to avoid duty, but to apprise Gunny Gutierrez of what he felt was a dangerous circumstance.

"Hamilton, I read you loud and clear. However, this is the United States Marine Corps, not the fucking Boy Scouts, and the captain has his reasons for needing reconnaissance to our southern flank. You're the hero, and your squad will run the checkpoints exactly as ordered. You will pick up a fire team of Ruff Puff [Vietnamese Army National Guardsmen were called Ruff Puffs by the American soldiers and Marines because of their English-language acronym: RFPF (Regional Forces Popular Forces)] interpreters on your way out through the ARVN camp. That is all!"

Gutierrez had fought in subzero weather for seventy-odd days and nights from the Chosin Reservoir in Korea in the First Marine Division's breakout against nine Chinese Communist divisions. The Marines had destroyed three divisions piecemeal and run the North Koreans back across the Yalu River. Gutierrez had been in tough battles without hot food or sleep. So he understood Luther Hamilton's position, but Marines always did what they were ordered to do! When it got down to realities, the mission always came first.

Luther Hamilton dragged himself into First Squad's hootch, at the front of a long row of plywood-sided, tin-roofed identical huts. The men of his squad were either crapped out on their bunks or moving around in slow motion like ghosts from the Lost Battalion (Marines killed in battle).

"Men, I pass along this order with great reluctance. Our commanding officer has ordered a sweep of the

Que Son Mountains scheduled to commence at eighteen hundred hours, or thirty minutes from now. Gunny Gutierrez just passed along the order. We're making a ten-klick recon patrol through several villages to check mainly for enemy movement and supplies. We will be gone all night. It's going to be a bitch and a half! Plus, the captain told Gunny Gutierrez to have us take along a squad of Ruff Puffs. Let's saddle up! Equipment check in ten minutes. Let's move, people."

"Fuck me if we ain't had a hard enough night to have to crawl up those elephant grass slopes," said PFC Burns. "I'm sorry, Luther, but this deal is really bullshit. The fucking Popular Forces' soldiers will bug out the first sign of Charlie. Let's leave the Ruff Puffs at home, man." Burns pretty well said what was on everyone's mind.

Luther maintained his stance. "I agree with all of you," he said. "We did plenty last night and we deserve a night off duty. However, from the captain's viewpoint he needs information before we kick off the big sweep into the Arizona next week. We cannot risk our security here at An Hoa if we are taking half the battalion out to the Song Thu Bon and chasing Charlie all week. First Squad must run a clean, thorough reconnaissance of the Que Son hamlets and trails before next week."

In ten minutes all the Marines in First Squad were loosely formed in the company street and had been joined by Lance Corporal Matarazzi and his ammunition bearer, PFC Jessmore. Everyone wore flak jackets and helmets, and carried an M-14 rifle. Mat had his

M-60 machine gun. Not one Marine wore his haversack, nor did any of the men carry more than two canteens. The squad would travel fast and light. This was
a reconnaissance patrol, and we were instructed to
observe Charlie, not to engage unless attacked or
forced to fight our way home. We were equipped to
defend ourselves, especially with an attached machine
gun team. We all wanted to forget the Popular Forces.

After equipment check, the squad moved out
through the southern portion of the airstrip and past
the Battalion Aid Station. Outside the barbed-wire
defenses of An Hoa Combat Base, we entered the
Popular Forces (PF) camp. The Ruff Puffs were fin-
ishing evening chow when we approached their commander, who had already been issued orders to
accompany us on patrol.

Luther said directly to the PF officer, "Sir, why
aren't your men ready to go? We have eight miles to
cover in mountainous terrain."

The Ruff Puff commanding officer was polite and
formal, and his English wasn't bad, either. "So sorry,
Corporal, but soldiers not finished eating. How long
you say patrol in mountain?"

"Sir, the patrol will take eight to ten hours, and we
must be leaving now if we are to surprise the enemy
during his nightly movements." Luther put the Puff
lieutenant directly on-line about our mission.

"Corporal, what you say about enemy movement?"
The PF officer was all ears now.

"Sir, we have orders to locate and destroy a Viet
Cong unit with North Vietnamese advisers that has

infiltrated the Que Son plateau." Luther stretched the truth that last bit a little too far.

The PF officer bit down hard. "Excuse me, Corporal, but my soldiers are only Popular Force. We are National Guard, have no training for combat against North Vietnamese Army regular soldiers. No, thank you, Corporal, we stay here in camp tonight."

Luther played with the Ruff Puff for the squad's enjoyment. "Sir, are you refusing the Marine commander's order to accompany our patrol into the Que Son Mountains tonight?"

The finality of the PF's leader was characteristic. "I am sorry, Corporal, but must decline to patrol with you. U.S. Marines always do pretty good by yourself anyway. Good luck."

Luther spun on his heel and shouted to First Squad for effect. "Saddle up, Marines, and prepare to move out to chase down and kill the Viet Cong dogs. Every man better have a sharpened bayonet on him. I want a count of VC ears when we get back to An Hoa. Let's go kill some Commies!"

Luther turned to the PF officer, who was squatting down with several of his soldiers. "Sir, with your permission, I am ready to take my men into the mountains to hunt the Communists. With your blessing, sir, we shall be successful and not lose too many of our Marines."

"You have my blessing, Corporal. Marines are very brave. Please save my country. Thank you." The PF officer was sincere. Of course, we never understood how he expected us to save his country if he wasn't willing to fight for it.

CHAPTER SIXTEEN

Night Patrol into the Jungle Hillside

First Squad formed a long column and moved out through the perimeter of the Popular Forces camp. The Marines followed small paddy dikes that led to a shallow, rock-lined streambed. Once the stream was forded, the topography changed drastically. Gone was the flat matrix of rice fields punctuated by tree lines grown by the villagers as windbreaks. No evenly tiered rice fields rose and fell with the gentle swells of the ground. This new landscape cut up into the foothills of the Que Son Range abruptly. The foliage was denser and the growth taller than that in the rice valley. Movement of the Marine column was greatly restricted, and the troops instinctively closed up the interval between men to about five meters. John Lafley was on point and had to negotiate the stubborn trail that wound far to port, then abruptly turned in a long cast to starboard. The main direction, however, was ever upward. Switchback trails with deep reversals only make the climber work harder. His real progress is decidedly less than he envisions.

After an hour of marching, during which the squad

covered ten feet for every foot gained in actual ascent, the first checkpoint was reached.

Luther Hamilton called our radio sign and position in to the company headquarters in An Hoa. Hamilton indicated the general direction of the next checkpoint to us by moving his knife hand down several times.

The patrol now became difficult. The trees, shrubs, and general undergrowth had grown considerably taller and thicker than at the base of the hillside. The point man was now struggling to break through foliage that had recently grown across the trail, impeding any progress, however small. Lafley was a veteran of the mountain campaigns the 2/5 had waged against the deadly NVA divisions pouring across the DMZ. One mountain trail was as difficult as the next, but Lafley had forgotten how difficult it was to move through terrain this thick.

Checkpoint Two was still a half hour's hard march away. Static crackled in the radio handset. Luther was handed the handset by Paul Blocker, who carried the PRC-10 radio strapped to his back.

As Luther lifted the handset to his mouth to transmit, the 105mm guns of the Eleventh Marines Artillery at An Hoa fired a six-gun battery, which was immediately followed by four more guns firing. This meant the six-howitzer battery had "fired for effect," and ten rounds of high-explosive 105mm artillery shells were flying in a lethal group into the star-studded night sky. The shells' trajectory would take them high into the air, then they would plunge onto the target. Fire support at An Hoa had probably plotted the harassment-and-interdiction fires earlier in the day, and the fire missions then had been approved by Battalion HQ. It could be that First Squad had been expected to reach Checkpoint Two before the concentration of 105mm shells was fired.

Hamilton threw the handset back to Blocker and yelled, "Everybody, hit the deck and stay down. Arty is on the way into our sector. Stay down and keep low."

A faint swishing noise could be heard very high in the air. The sound grew until a distinct roar could be plainly heard coming straight for our position.

"Jesus, man, listen to that shit coming down right at us," Paul Blocker said, giving voice to every man's fears.

The roar had increased to a thunderous pitch, as though a whole trainload of huge diesel engines had broken loose at full throttle and had turned around, heading back to the station.

"God in Heaven, we'll all be killed!" Lafley screamed. The words were muted by the power of the now shrieking shells as they descended almost on top of First Squad's unprotected position.

The huge shells impacted fifty meters from First Squad, almost at the top of the hillock. The shells passed over First Squad and inscribed a fiery path of black and red explosions down the far hillside and into the small village nestled at the bottom of the draw. Shrapnel sung up the hill as it sliced its lethal way over and through First Squad's prostrate Marines.

"I'm hit in the arm, man. This shit burns like crazy. Get it out of me!" Paul Blocker cried out in the aftermath of the first volley. More would soon follow.

Luther was instantly on his feet. "Culbertson, get on the point and get us out of here."

"Okay, I got the point. I am going to our right to get away from this village in case they fire again." I offered an alternative to reversing our course, since it appeared the village had been designated as the target by the Eleventh Marine's gunners back at battalion. It was logical to sidestep to the right and get out of the path of the second salvo rather than to reverse our path and try to run back under it. It would be fatal to go forward; the next concentration would likely increase range and straddle the village, killing any enemy troops flushed out of hiding by the first strike.

I got to the head of the column and began to jog off to our right flank, picking up a narrow footpath as we rounded the side of the hill. We were not exposed to direct firing from this angle. I felt certain we would be out of harm's way as long as we continued to descend and drift to our right flank.

The guns of the 105mm artillery battery down the slopes in An Hoa Combat Base fired again. I clearly saw the muzzle flashes of the six howitzers as their tilted barrels saluted the black expanse of night. The guns fired in sequence, sending steel-cased warheads the size of small saplings hurtling high, then downward toward our hastily abandoned previous entrapment.

The Marines of First Squad turned in amazement as the next flight of shells slammed to earth on the far side of the village. Viet Cong would be blown apart as they fled the temporary shelter of the village. The darkness had descended like a shroud over the patrol, and my only focus was on the trail ahead.

Luther said, "Culbertson, stay right and gain some elevation so we can take another bearing on an azimuth to An Hoa." Moving sideways and descending was distorting his perspective on the location of our combat base.

"Hamilton, I'm going to climb straight up this next slope and look-see. We ought to be nearly on top of An Hoa." My last vantage point had led me to believe that the base was half a klick to the right and a couple of miles straight down the mountain.

I knew we were in trouble after the first ten yards up the slope. I had pushed my body into a tall stand of dense grasses that appeared to stretch all the way to the top of the hill. I forced my leaning torso into the stand of grass, straining with my muscles and churning my legs to no avail. We had hit an extensive patch of elephant grass. The plants stood as tall as ten feet, and the broad leaves were edged with deep serrations that extended the length of the leaves. These sharp edges caught hold of clothing and skin and produced long, deep cuts and scratches in everything they contacted. I could not pierce the wall of elephant grass by attempting to charge through it.

I raised my M-14 rifle above my head and fell like a book toppling off a shelf into the clump of grass. I used my body weight and leverage to push the grasses down and then, rising to my knees, crawled up the bent grasses until I could stand and repeat the process.

"Hamilton, the next man after me has to close the interval or this elephant grass will snap back erect. This is going to kill me, but I'm breaking a trail to the top. Everyone else keep up and smash this stuff flat," I pleaded with the troops behind me.

Up and down I went making a weird rhythm like some primitive mud dog powering out of a bog, only to land back on its face prostrate and make another try. After forty-five minutes of steady exertion, I crawled to my feet bleeding and bruised. I stared into the clear night air at the dazzling display of lights down in the rice valley several miles below. I had done it! An Hoa was nearby now, and a straight course down the mountain would take us directly into the southwest section of the Marine lines.

But we had forgotten about the dreaded fire support missions that were being plotted back at battalion. Furthermore, in our haste to escape the last fusillade, we had abandoned our checkpoint route entirely. Luther got back on the radio.

He said we were lost somewhere southwest of the base, about two klicks into the Que Son Mountains. He left out the part about the Eleventh Marine's H & I fire mission, which had almost put First Squad into the ground.

Luther was told there was another fire mission in our sector and to hold position and get down in defilade (using the terrain for protection) if possible. Luther and the rest of us were having serious trouble believing this nonsense.

"Culbertson," he said, "after they fire the barrage get your butt on the point and don't look back till we're the hell out of this mess." Luther wanted to get the squad high-stepping back down the slopes. Then he'd look up the Eleventh Marines who'd planned this caper and skin their hides.

"I will be hightailing it down the mountain, Luther," I said. "That is, unless this next fire mission blows the tails off of all of us." I found it hard to be overly optimistic, especially when our own Marines reacted this way.

The big guns echoed down at the Eleventh Marine's fire support pits. We bunched together in a shallow ravine that faced the guns. The roar of the shells became audible within the first twenty seconds after firing. Then the noise of the incoming ordnance increased in amplitude and shrillness. An earsplitting thunderous whine descended on our squad where we nestled together like a covey of helpless quail warding off a hunter's advance.

The shells crashed to earth and detonated on impact. The line of exploding canisters began a hundred yards over our heads, near the peak of our mountain. The explosions walked right up the mountain's flank and held the jungle-crowned summit with a fiery embrace. The elephant grass caught fire, then smoldered, and great chunks of burning leaves and other plant debris floated into the gusting winds that fanned the slopes.

"Culbertson, get us out of here! Right now, Marine! Everybody saddle up. We're heading for An Hoa nonstop. High-stepping now! Let's move out, point." Everybody had taken plenty of this horseshit by then. The next fire mission could take us off the mountain like smashed ants. Lady Luck was out on the other side of town that night!

I increased my speed from a fast march to a quick-time jog. The shrubs and bushes flew by us. No one broke an ankle or twisted a knee, but a couple of us had shrapnel wounds that were growing painful. Unlike anywhere else I have been, in Vietnam the tropical heat and dampness caused a seriously high rate of infection, and shrapnel wounds became infected quickly.

The lights of An Hoa were directly in front of us, and living through that artillery nightmare began to seem possible. We tossed out a yellow smoke grenade and yelled toward the lines that a Marine patrol was coming in. Gary Woodruff passed that night's password, "Crimson Tide," to the Marine sentry who challenged him, and he had Gary advance to be recognized. After he determined that Gary wasn't Charlie, I was allowed to escort the rest of the squad through the Marine bunkers into An Hoa Combat Base.

Half the squad retired to our company area for the night, and I led a contingent of three Marines to the naval dispensary, where our wounds were treated. Shrapnel was removed from my elbow, which was cut to the bone and required a dozen stitches. I was kept for four days in the infirmary while my temperature hovered at 104 degrees, sending me into a delirium. I also received the Purple Heart, but was glad to still be with the living.

We later found out that some of the explosions that had grazed the top of our first hill were actually enemy mortar fire. Evidently, Charlie had his tubes set up, and when the H and I fires illuminated our position, he added some icing to our cake.

The plunging 105mm shells of the first barrage

walked into the village, and most of that shrapnel carried downslope away from our position. However, the forward observer at An Hoa had noticed secondary explosions coinciding with the last four Marine rounds and impacting upon the top of the hill, where the bulk of the 105mm shells had landed on their way toward the village. The secondary explosions that walked from the hilltop down onto us were enemy mortar rounds fired from a position opposite An Hoa. Our patrol had been caught in the crossing fires.

Sometimes everything just goes right! We prayed that another patrol of this general nature (FUBAR) did not happen again in our lifetimes.

PART TWO: Operation TUSCALOOSA

CHAPTER SEVENTEEN

Frag Order

After we returned from the night patrol, all hands hit the sack. We were given the next day off to repair our 782 web gear and clean and service our rifles, uniforms, and—not least of all—ourselves. The Marine Corps generally granted its returning warriors time to mend before the next battle—especially when the troops had been pushed hard with little sleep. Lightly injured Marines also used this downtime to visit the infirmary. Finally, we went to the battalion mess hall for some well-deserved hot chow. And, of course, nothing tasted better than a fresh cigarette after a good meal.

At First Marine Division Headquarters at Da Nang, the General Staff had drawn up an operations plan for another search-and-destroy mission. The operation would be of approximate battalion strength, an attempt to destroy the Viet Cong Regional Headquarters in the Arizona Territory northwest of An Hoa. The operation was code-named TUSCALOOSA and was scheduled to commence on January 24, 1967, at 0730 hours.

SECRET

Headquarters
2nd Battalion, 5th Marines
1st Marine Division (Rein) FMF
FPO San Francisco, California 96602

3/JBS/jcv
20 Jan 1967
003A2067

To: Commanding General, 1st Marine Division
From: Commanding Officer, 2nd Battalion, 5th Marines
Subj: Operational Plan, Organizational Table
Ref: (a) 2nd Bn, 5th Marine Frag Order 2-67
        (b) Maps, ANS Series L7014, Vietnam 1:50,000,
             Sheet 66401V

1. Code Names "TUSCALOOSA" (Search and Destroy)
2. Date of Operations: 240730H Jan 1967 to 281800H
                     Jan 1967 or Until terminated
3. Location: QUAN DUY XUYEN South Vietnam. Coordinates bordered on the west by NSGL AT91, on the east by NSGL AT00, on the north by the SONG THU BON River, on the south by NSGL AT50.
4. <u>Control and Command Headquarters</u>

<u>2nd Battalion, (-) (Reinforced),</u>	Lt. Col. W.C.
<u>5th Marines</u>	AIRHEART
Company Headquarters & Supply	Capt. A.J. BOCCUTI
Company F (Reinforced)	Capt. G.S. BURGETT
Company H (Reinforced)	Capt. J.J. DOHERTY JR.
2nd Plt (Rein) Co. E Sparrow Hawk #2	Lt. P.C. BERTOLOZZI
3rd Plt (Rein) Co. G Sparrow Hawk #1	SSgt. W.M. CARTER

5. <u>Task Organization</u>

<u>2nd Battalion (-) (Rein), 5th Marines</u>	Lt. Col. W.C. AIRHEART
H&S Co. (-)	Capt. A.J. BOCCUTI
E Battery, 11th Marines	
DET., 1st Tank Bn	
DET., Scout Dog Plt	
<u>Company F (Reinforced)</u>	Capt. G.S. BURGETT
FO Team	
FAC Team	
Scout Dog Team	
Interpreter	
S-2	

SECRET

Company H (Reinforced)   Capt. J.J. DOHERTY JR.

FO Team
FAC Team
Scout Dog Team
Interpreter
S-2 Scouts

2nd Platoon Co. E Sparrow Hawk #2   Lt. P.C. BERTO-
FO Team   LOZZI

3rd Platoon Co. G. Sparrow Hawk #1   SSgt. W.M. CARTER
FO Team

6. Supporting Arms
    (a) Air strike from Da Nang Marine Air Base
        (1) The tactical Air Request net utilized during Operation Tuscaloosa will be BUTTON CRIMSON FM. All requesting traffic will relay through An Hoa. 14 (Rear). All air strikes will be run on BUTTON COLD 1, or BUTTON TRUST UHF.
        The Medevac personnel will be handled by the Resupply/Medevac helicopters stationed at An Hoa. The Sparrow Hawk CH-46's will be utilized for Medevac extraction. The average time for Medevac completion should be 25 minutes. Two Sparrow Hawks will be utilized during the operation. The average time from request to insertion is anticipated to be one hour.
    (b) Artillery
        (1) Two guns from E-2-11 will be helilifted into MY LOC 2 for the operation. They will be able to function as an independent unit. It is suggested that these guns have at least 2,000 rounds at their position.
        Company commanders are reminded that if they want Artillery fired while an adjoining unit is running an Air Strike, or a Medevac Mission, artillery will have to wait until the air is clear. It is highly recommended that unit commanders reach mutual agreement, prior to the operation's onset, as to which supporting arm they will lean on; Air or artillery. When a clear choice exists it is pointed out to Commanders that while air support can deliver heavier ordnance, artillery is capable of maintaining fire over a longer period of time. In this regard, it is recommended that artillery fire missions be utilized at all times unless supporting arms such as Napalm are necessary.

                     A.J. BOCCUTI
                     By Direction

SECRET

2nd Battalion, 5th Marines
An Hoa, Vietnam
20 January 1967

Frag Order 02-67 (Operation Tuscaloosa)
Ref: (a) Maps South Vietnam 1:50,000 Sheet 66401V
Time Zones: H

<u>TASK ORGANIZATION</u>: No Changes
1. SITUATION
    a. Enemy Forces: Viet Cong, Main Forces, Guer-
                               rillas, North Vietnamese Advi-
                               sors
    b. Friendly Forces: 2/5(-) (Rein) Companies
    c. Attachments and Detachments. No change except
        addition of Detachment Scout Dogs (4 dogs) with
        handlers.
2. MISSION
    2/5 (-) (Rein) conducts Search and Destroy operations
    in NE sector of TAOR bounded on the North and West
    by the SONG THU BON River, on the East by the rail-
    road, on the South by the East-West main road.
3. EXECUTION
    a. Concept of Operations: Commencing D-day minus
        one, 2/5 (Rein) moves to line of departure positions
        and prepares for Search & Destroy operation in
        Northeast sector of TAOR on D-day to locate,
        destroy, and or capture enemy forces, supplies,
        equipment, and documents.
    b. Company "H & S" Commencing D-day minus one
        (230730H Jan 67) move via LVT's to MY LOC 2
        vicinity AT915515 and PHU LOC 6 vicinity
        AT928527 with Battalion Command Group and
        security forces necessary to maintain these two CP
        locations during period of operation.
    c. Company "H"s Commencing D-day minus one,
        when relieved by Company "H&S", will move to line
        of departure vicinity AT955346 and establish
        patrol base for the night of D-day minus one. On
        D-day commence sweep South and East to Search &
        Destroy and link up with company "F" on order.
        D-day plus two, or on order sweep back to CP (Com-
        mand Post) PHU LOC 6.
    d. Company "F"s Commencing D-day minus one.
        (230730H) (23 January at 0730 Hours a.m.) move
        to line of departure vicinity AT P975517 and estab-
        lish patrol base for the night of D-day minus one.
        On D-day commence sweep North and East to
        Search and Destroy and link up with Company "H"
        on order. D-day plus one, conduct sweep to
        AT9754, AT9852, and AT9952. D-day, plus two, or
        on order sweep back to CP An Hoa.

SECRET

Gary Woodruff (*left*) and Alfred McKnight at An Hoa Combat Base after a patrol.

CH-46 Sea Knight helicopter of the kind used during Operation Tuscaloosa to evacuate casualties and insert Sparrow Hawk reinforcements.

Squad leader Luther Hamilton (*left*) and his team at the firebase at Nong Son Mountain in the heart of the Arizona Territory.

John Matarazzi (*left*) and Stephan Gedzyk, the two best M-60 gunners in the 2nd Battalion, at An Hoa, 1967.

An Hoa runway with control tower in rear. Hootches are lined up on company streets.

George Heeman and Alfred McKnight happy
just to be alive after Tuscaloosa, 1967.

Point Scout John Lafley.
A Salish Indian from Montana,
Lafley was a natural in the jungle.

Stephan Gedzyk, 3rd Platoon M-60 machine-gunner who was instrumental to the Hotel attack on La Bac village on Operation Tuscaloosa.

The command post bunker on Phu Loc 6 firebase that was used by Lieutenant Colonel Airheart during Operation Tuscaloosa.

Platoon Sergeant McDonald, a Silver Star winner, and squad leader Luther Hamilton at An Hoa Combat Base, 1967.

Squad leader Sergeant Manuel Ybarra. We called him Yogi Bear. Ybarra fought desperately to save Pfc. Cross, who was wounded in his bunker on the Song Thu Bon blocking force.

Corporal Smaltz (*left*) and John Lafley (*center*) with another Marine at the An Hoa enlisted men's club, 1967.

Pfc. Marvin Redeye, 3rd Platoon scout and Cheyenne warrior, on the back side of Nong Son Mountain, 1967.

The boys at Phu Loc 6 after Tuscaloosa, 1967:
(*left to right*) Corporal Kirby, Sergeant Ybarra, Sergeant
McDonald, Lance Corporal Hamilton.

The Operation Tuscaloosa crossing point, circled. Hotel's
2nd and 3rd Platoons crossed the Thu Bon River and were
ambushed and pinned down on the sandbar. Enemy troops
were dug in to the riverbank on the right, overlooking the
sandbar where Hotel took so many casualties.

Third Platoon, Hotel Company fires a 106 mm recoilless rifle off Nong Son Mountain into the Arizona Territory, Second Lieutenant Pindel (*squatting*) in command.

Lance Corporal Luther Hamilton prepares chow on Non Song Mountain, 1967.

Six miles north of An Hoa, Hotel Company Gunnery Sergeant Husak (*forefront*) halts patrol before reaching the Thu Bon River off Liberty Bridge.

Lance Corporal Luther Hamilton at M-60 position overlooking the Arizona Territory, off Nong Son Mountain, 1967.

Jerome J. Doherty (later, as a captain, commanding officer of Hotel Company) is seen here as a lieutenant on his second tour in Vietnam. Doherty, a brave and skilled combat officer, won the Silver Star Medal for action during Tuscaloosa.

The author receiving his third Purple Heart Medal from Colonel Nat M. Pace, Commanding Officer, Marine Barracks, Subic Bay, Philippines.

SECRET

    e. Company "E": Provide one alert platoon (Rein) to be located at An Hoa on D-day minus one to reinforce either maneuvering company on order.

    f. Company "F": Provide one alert platoon (Rein) to be located at An Hoa on D-day minus one to reinforce either maneuvering company on order.

    g. <u>Coordinating Instructions</u>:

        (1) D-day - 24 January 1967.

        (2) H hour - TBD (To be determined).

        (3) Direct Liaison is authorized between maneuvering companies.

        (4) After link up of Co. "H" and Co. "F" consolidate night defenses.

        (5) Two 105mm guns to be prepositioned MY LOC 2 on D-day minus one.

        (6) Request for Air and Arty through 2/5 FSCC An Hoa.

        (7) Two Med Evac and two resupply choppers located at An Hoa.

4.   ADMINISTRATION AND LOGISTICS

    a. Spot Reports as required.

    b. Each individual Marine to carry six (6) MCI's and two canteens water plus purification tablets. Resupply as required.

5.   COMMAND AND COMMUNICATIONS

    a. Battalion CP located PHU LOC 6 vicinity AT928527.

    b. <u>Communications</u>. No Change. Relay facilities to be established at PHU LOC 6.

W.C. AIRHEART
LIEUTENANT COLONEL, U.S. MARINE CORPS
COMMANDING

ANNEXES:
    A - (Operation Overlay) to Frag Order 02-67
DISTRIBUTION: A
    Commanding General, 1st Marine Division (3)

SECRET

CHAPTER EIGHTEEN

D Day Minus Two

On January 22, 1967, orders were passed to platoon commanders, platoon sergeants, and squad leaders. The general facts of the mission were disseminated to the companies, and word was given to the troops. The operational order is always fragmented as it reaches each lower echelon of command (frag order). The general staff at division headquarters had drawn up the specifics in the operational plan. Battalion headquarters issued Frag Order 02-67, which gave operational orders to the companies that would take the field in Operation TUSCALOOSA. Foxtrot Company, Hotel Company, Echo Company Sparrow Hawk Platoon, and Golf Company Sparrow Hawk Platoon gave specific orders to the platoon commanders, who informed their respective platoons of their mission.

It has never been a characteristic of any Marine unit to divulge any more of the "big picture" than is necessary for an individual unit to perform its duty. This ancient military practice is referred to as the "need to know" principle, and adhering to it means that if any details of the battle plan are not critical to a unit's function they are not revealed. Needless to say, the only real information made available to the Marine rifleman preparing for Operation TUSCALOOSA pertained to the gear he was to pack. The gear requirement specified numbers of everything from halozone and salt tablets to bullets, canteens, C rations, and extra ammunition such as mortar rounds and LAWs rocket tubes. Rifle platoons spent the day preparing their equipment and standing rifle inspection for their platoon leaders and platoon sergeants.

Scuttlebutt about destinations and specific targets Division had in mind was all over the map. Rumors circulated about a new main force battalion that had entered our sector of operations in the Arizona Territory. This same rumor placed the Viet Cong regulars and their North Vietnamese advisers directly in the path of the 2/5's sweep route along the Song Thu Bon ten klicks northwest of An Hoa. All the companies in the battalion had patrolled the river's meanders and the rice paddies of Duc Duc Province on many occasions. A fight was coming and the officers and staff NCOs of the 2/5 had the edge on Charlie in training, experience, and—as far as we were concerned—courage.

The men of First Squad stowed their gear and lumbered off to evening chow. When Hotel crossed An Hoa's airstrip and perimeter wire and entered the paddy-scaped water world of Arizona, we knew the game would be for blood.

CHAPTER NINETEEN

D Day Minus One—
"The Tunnel"

Morning broke through gray, scudding clouds in the distance. No rain had fallen, but the air was laden with moisture. A clammy chill permeated the ranks and made the stiff protective plates in our flak jacket panels feel heavy as metal. Everyone had red mud caked on the leather uppers of their jungle boots, which did not keep out the wet or cold as the Marines ran the river trails and paddy dikes.

Under the command of Captain Doherty, Hotel Company moved out along the An Hoa strip and down the line of bunkers to the perimeter-wire defenses. The mood of the troops was different from the last patrol. The Marines of Hotel had a seriousness about them on this bleak morning. Everyone knew we weren't going out to take a census of the population.

The column assumed a serpentine shape extending down the road through the rice fields toward the first huts of the Vietnamese village Luther Hamilton had escaped from on the night he made that heroic dash back to Phu Loc 6. No hostility or contraband was found as the squads fanned out through the village.

Ahead lay an immense spreading mosaic of rectangular fields mostly filled with rainwater. The fields seemed to disappear into the thick jungle that covered the hills in the distance.

The point fire team carefully made its way up dike levies and onto the winding, narrow, dirt trails that separated the rice fields. The point scouts knew how easy it was to lull yourself into a complacent spirit, fanned by the natural scenic beauty of the landscape. Even so, it took the explosion of a booby trap or mine to jerk some day-trippers back to reality. The scouts with any time in-country had all seen the mutilated remains of point men who had gotten lax or allowed themselves to become distracted. The lucky ones were just maimed, although some were so horribly crippled that few would call them lucky.

One of the point men yelled back toward the platoon commander, "We got ourselves a bunker complex here behind this last hut. Looks like it runs back under the village." The sighting was repeated down the length of the column until it reached the lieutenant in command of Third Platoon, on the point.

Lieutenant Smith was new in the field but had no problem with handling this obstacle. "Where is PFC Jessmore?" the lieutenant yelled down the line.

PFC Jessmore was an ammunition bearer who usually served on John Matarazzi's machine gun crew. He was also the shortest, lightest, and perhaps the gutsiest Marine in Hotel Company. Armed with only a .45 caliber pistol, Jessmore routinely took a crooked G.I. flashlight and descended into the labyrinthine darkness of newly found tunnel complexes.

Jessmore dropped his flak jacket, helmet, and haversack and ran toward the platoon commander's position, ready to play his deadly rendition of "Tunnel Rat."

"Sir, the lieutenant wanted me, sir?" Jessmore's expression betrayed how intensely he anticipated a mission.

"PFC Jessmore, the point team has located a bunker entrance to the rear of the last hut up the trail. I want you to enter the complex only so far as you feel mobile and in control. I want to give the company commander an estimate of the bunker's size and dimensions before we bring up the engineers. Don't be too ambitious down there! We have other business with the Viet Cong that takes precedence over this activity. Got it?"

"Sir, yes sir! They haven't killed me down in them tunnels yet, sir. I got a special feel for this type of problem, sir." Without further formality, PFC Jessmore unbuttoned and tossed aside his olive-green jungle utility top. Wearing only trousers and jungle boots, with his pistol holstered and a flashlight in his hand, Jessmore approached the point team and checked out the tunnel mouth.

"Looks like it runs under that dirt mound and probably descends under the village itself. I'll check it out. If I ain't back here in ten minutes, send Gedzyk after me." Jessmore ducked his head into the opening that gaped out of the ground in a thicket of jungle plants and foliage. His knees tucked up, then he pushed his body into the hole and out of view.

Inside, the tunnel was a straight shaft that ran back

under the mounds of earth behind the huts. Then the slope increased, and Jessmore crawled downward at a 30-degree angle. The walls of this part of the passageway were shored up by stout timbers that supported the earthen ceiling like an old mine shaft. Jessmore noted distances as he moved. Water droplets slid down the beams onto Jessmore's arms as he squeezed through inch by inch. Just as Jessmore began to think the tunnel was empty, the corridor turned abruptly to the left, back under the Vietnamese village itself. The tunnel widened until Jessmore could stand hunched over and shine his light into the enormous cavity that spread itself before him.

"Holy Toledo, just look at this place, will ya?" Jessmore said in a whisper to no one in particular. His eyes ran over the cots, bunk beds, tables, and folding chairs that were strewn over an amphitheater-size room that smelled sharply of tincture of iodine. A closer examination revealed tangles of gauze and bandages haphazardly tossed on cots and tables recently evacuated of their patients. Medicine bottles, intravenous tubing, and a metal table full of surgical implements glittered as the bright arc of Jessmore's flashlight scanned the farther reaches of the hospital.

Searching right, Jessmore's light picked up two glowing orbs against the far wall. Jessmore placed his right hand on the grip of his pistol, sliding the barrel free of its holster and drawing a tight bead with the front sight post on the gleaming crystals. He thumbed the pistol off safety and took up the trigger slack, ready to fire.

"*Chieu hoi, chieu hoi,* Marine!" Two stumps that

had once been arms shot straight into the darkness. A worn green battle jacket, its sleeves caked with dried blood, covered the arms. The stumps of the wrists were covered by dressings of discolored cloth and stank of iodine. As Jessmore moved closer, the Viet Cong soldier's face froze in the beam of the Marine's flashlight. His coal-black eyes were moist with tears, and he nodded his head up and down in relief that his life might be spared.

Jessmore holstered his pistol and, without taking his eyes off the Viet Cong soldier, edged up to the man until he stood directly in front of him. Jessmore could see that the soldier's hands had been surgically repaired after some mishap that had mangled one and blown the other off entirely.

"Well, old partner, you look like your buddies deserted your ass and left you for the Marines to eat. Don't your officers tell you Marines eat their prisoners? Ain't that so, boy? Well, I ain't goin' to eat ya, nor kill ya. Okay!" Jessmore suddenly remembered that the platoon commander had said they needed to interrogate prisoners to help find Charlie. This guy would be a prime source of information if he lived.

"Come on, fella! Let's get out of here. Okay? You are with PFC Jessmore! Ace-number-one tunnel rat. Everything's gonna be okay. You jus' follow me out."

When Jessmore broke out of the tunnel entrance, a cheer went up from Third Platoon. Then the Viet Cong soldier emerged and everyone cocked their rifles because they were caught off guard. Jessmore straightened out the mess as soon as he caught his breath. "Shit, man, there's a whole damn hospital down there. Surgery, a hundred beds, medicine, everything, and this one dude that they left behind. He ain't got no hands, and his sorry-assed buddies left him behind to die. Hell, I kinda like him 'cause he didn't put up no fight or even try to escape. Somebody get the lieutenant over here. I'll make a map of this tunnel. Charlie will be in deep shit when we blow this baby! Where's the damn engineers when you need 'em, man?"

PFC Jessmore was high on adrenaline, but he knew he had done a righteous job. He could get a promotion out of this tunnel caper. "Lance Corporal Jessmore" sure had a good sound. Jessmore was snatched out of his reverie by Lieutenant Smith, who came forward with four engineers carrying olive drab web packs full of C-4 high explosive.

Lieutenant Smith spoke first: "Jessmore, outline the general configuration of the main bunker. I want charges dug into the roof so that we can collapse it." He turned to the staff sergeant who headed up the engineering detail.

"That'll work, sir," said the sergeant. "We also need to look for the exit corridor somewhere along the general direction your tunnel rat followed. If we don't close the entire complex off, sir, Charlie will have a much easier time reconstructing it."

Lieutenant Smith was quick to confirm the engineer's reasoning. "Sergeant," he said, "you have the liberty to detonate this tunnel as you see fit. My Marines will assist you in excavating holes to place the explosive charges. Carry on."

"Thank you, sir. We can accomplish this project in about an hour if all hands take care of business, sir."

PFC Jessmore had paced off the measurements he had taken as he crawled inside the tunnel shafts. He drove sticks into the ground to mark the general outline of the hospital and used more sticks to show the correct directions of the corridors and their doglegs. After forty-five minutes of digging, the engineer placed the charges in series—one charge wired to the next by det cord (detonation cord). Each brick of C-4 was bundled with a blasting cap that was pushed securely into the plastic explosive. The det cord fed into the blasting cap, which was then crimped down by the engineers. Another length of det cord trailed off to the next buried charge, where it was crimped into another blasting cap. A half dozen charges were laid that way, with separate explosives thrust into the entrance and the exit of the complex. In all, thirty-two bricks of C-4 were buried above the roof of the eighty-foot-long main operating room and dormitory.

Then the engineers herded the Marines back two hundred paces from the tunnel's center and all the men got down into the prone position as the staff sergeant in charge of the engineers bent over several control boxes with raised plungers.

"Fire in the hole! Fire in the hole!" the staff sergeant shouted in a voice loud enough for all hands to hear. He pressed the first plunger, and the charge went off at the tunnel entrance. The next plunger detonated the six charges along the hospital roof. The explosions echoed in series, one close after the other, until the ground over the hospital caved in, sending a cloud of dirt and debris high into the air, covering the Marines with dust and dirt. The explosion was so powerful that the shock wave collapsed the exterior walls of the two closest huts, leaving the thatched roofs flattened on the remains of the foundations.

Lieutenant Smith addressed his Marines. "All right, men," he said, "outstanding job there. Jessmore just might find himself a lance corporal when we get back. Saddle up! Lafley and Culbertson, get on the point and get us out of here. Head northeast toward the river, where we will set up a perimeter for the night. Watch out for mines and booby traps. Move out!"

CHAPTER TWENTY

D Day Minus One— "The Perimeter"

Lafley guided Third Platoon, followed in trace by Second and First Platoons. About two hundred Marines, including the CP (Command Post) Group and attached 60mm mortar teams, scout dog teams, and interpreter teams with their Kit Carson Scouts, were strung out along the many rice field dikes and trails weaving their way inextricably closer to the riverine sanctuary, Charlie's retreat.

After three hours' march, Hotel Company could identify the Marines of Foxtrot Company coming into a parallel column marching on Hotel's left flank. Foxtrot had reached the linkup point with Hotel Company by following the Song Thu Bon's meanders beginning at a point east of the firebase at Phu Loc 6. Hotel had traveled through the villages clustered north of An Hoa along the matrix of giant rice paddies extending far to the northeast into the heart of Arizona Territory. Now the sister companies of the 2/5 had linked up in a single, fast-moving column four hundred and fifty Marines strong.

The battalion commander had taken his command

post from An Hoa and transferred his staff to Phu Loc 6. From the command bunker at Phu Loc 6, Colonel Airheart would be "on the net" directing the movement of the three Marine companies that would be maneuvering for the kill directly on top of Charlie's riverside headquarters: Foxtrot Company and Hotel Company would be supported by H&S (Headquarters and Service) Company, which would deploy the larger organic weapons, such as 81mm mortars, and organize resupply missions for rations, ammunition, medical supplies, medevac, demolition engineers, and corpsmen.

An hour before dark, the two reinforced rifle companies split off to the north and south a mile from the river. Hotel and Foxtrot would pull their Marines into a series of elongated platoon-size defensive perimeters with the flanks of each ellipse in close proximity to its neighbor. The companies positioned their six platoons in a wide scimitar-shaped swath covering a half mile facing the river.

The company commanders sent orders to the platoon leaders to run looping ambush patrols toward the river to set up in cover a thousand meters to the front of the light battalion. Each ambush team had four or five Marines. All the ambush teams carried PRC-10 radios and were to contact the command post of their company at fifteen-minute intervals by keying their mikes a fixed number of times. Keying of the ambush teams' radios would be heard as a series of squelch-breaks at the company CP. If no squelch-break signal was heard by a company for a specific team, then the team that was to have sent the corresponding number of squelch-breaks was dead or had a broken radio.

Individual Marines were also sent outside the perimeter to stand four-hour listening posts (LPs). These troops had no radios. They carried only their rifles and a big set of "balls." If the listening post Marine wondered what he was supposed to listen for, the answer was simple. Nothing! His platoon was waiting for him to scream, if attacked, which would call the platoon to instant 100 percent alert.

Lieutenant Smith walked into First Squad's area, where all hands were busying themselves digging fighting holes for the night's defenses. The lieutenant looked his men over. "Culbertson, I want you to take your rifle and six magazines and proceed one hundred paces to your port flank," he said. "Find a hole or obstacle to sit behind and keep the field to our direct front under observation for any sign of the enemy until twenty-four-hundred hours. At twenty-four-hundred hours you will be replaced by PFC Burns, who will be the LP until oh-four-hundred hours. At oh-four-hundred hours PFC Blocker will assume the post until daybreak. Corporal Hamilton will post the LPs. I want to make the situation clear, men. We have ambush teams a klick to your front. You will not open fire unless attacked or fired upon. Good luck. Stay alert. Carry on!"

I grabbed my gear and checked my magazine pouches to make sure I had six full magazines, one in each pouch. Dusk was growing across the fields to our front, and darkness would fall over the landscape like a curtain in the next half hour. When my visibility was reduced to fifty feet or less, I collected my gear and rifle and checked out with Luther Hamilton, my squad leader.

"Luther, I'm going on out to man the LP. I'll be fifty meters to our oblique [at a 45-degree angle] front. If I see some activity, what do I do?" I asked, wanting Hamilton to direct my movements.

"If you are fired upon, return fire, and we'll send a team out to bring you in. If you get movement, do not fire unless the enemy is on top of your position. If any incoming mortars hit near you, stay down, and we'll bring you in when the firing lifts." Hamilton knew I could handle the LP with no problem.

"See you later. I'll be coming in at twenty-four-hundred hours. Pass the word to the sentries on the lines for me. *Buenas noches, caballeros!*" With that flourish of high school Spanish, I walked down the perimeter lines and out into the field to our front. A ditch ran off to my right flank, and I followed it twenty yards to the right flank of First Squad's position. I observed the surroundings in the gully, which was shallow enough for my head to just peer over the berm into the field. I moved forward fifty meters into the plowed dirt field, then stepped into a small defilade, the bottom of the undulating fold in the field's surface, which would provide cover and concealment for most of my body if I sat cross-legged.

I sat in a position that roughly imitated the Marine Corps' rifleman training sitting position, cross-legged with my torso leaning forward to observe my direct front. I slowly and methodically cast my vision from left to right and back again. I had soon memorized the main terrain features of the pasture, a sparse tree line a hundred meters farther ahead and a rising slope to my right that formed the foot of a long, low hill that stretched into the distance.

I kept my M-14 rifle across my knees with a round in the chamber, ready to fire. I wore my flak jacket and helmet. I realized the helmet would define my silhouette, so I finally removed it and put it behind me, then leaned back against the inside helmet liner. Looking for movement, not a particular object, I was reclining and scanning the field when something moved to my front. I thought I was seeing things, when the object I had in focus let out a low "Moooo. Moooo." The shape came into better focus even though the night had grown dark. A large herd of cattle was moving very slowly across the field from my left flank toward the platoon's perimeter. I could make out white cattle shapes and darker shapes numbering about a dozen at most. A cowbell gonged once, twice, three times, and I raised my body from my small fold of protective earth to get a clearer perspective. I had no sooner thrust myself into the clear night air than several automatic weapons fired short bursts in my direction. The bullets ricocheted off the dirt and threw chunks of sod and rocks into my face. The Viet Cong had concealed themselves behind the cattle in the herd until I moved, and then they had opened fire.

I grabbed my rifle and helmet with one hand and with the other pushed myself into a crouch. When the bursts of fire subsided, I thrust myself from my hole and ran in a weaving S for the ditch to my rear. The bullets ripped up the pasture, trailing behind my driving boots. I tumbled headlong into a ditch and crashed shoulders-first into a green stand of young bamboo. The bamboo thicket was composed of trees that were from three to five inches thick. The bamboo was so stout that it hardly trembled as I smashed into it. I was still lying on my back, breathing deeply and wondering if my shoulders were collapsed, when a team of Marines moved into the ditch next to me.

"Hold on, Culbertson. We're going to put some M-79 grenades out in the field," explained one Marine, evidently the fire-team leader. A Marine with an M-79 grenade launcher stepped up to the bank of the ditch and fired a round into the general area where the muzzle flashes of the AK-47 rifles had been visible from First Squad's perimeter vantage point. The 40mm grenade flew far enough to arm itself before exploding violently in the field. The M-79 man launched grenade after grenade, saturating the area where the enemy fire had originated. The field was lit up like downtown Saigon as the grenades burst one after another, throwing curtains of deadly shrapnel across the textured dirt pasture.

Charlie, as usual, was way ahead of the Marines' counterfire. The Viet Cong infantrymen had already pulled back to the tree line at the far end of the field, so several of the Marines stepped out of the ditch to check the effectiveness of their fusillade of grenade fire.

As I looked over the lip of the ditch that had sheltered me from the grazing fire of the Viet Cong, a

Marine, M-79 grenade launcher in his hand, stood up in front of me to survey the damage he had wrought with his weapon. He turned and spoke to the fire-team leader, "Guess that ran Charlie's ass out of here. This little M-79 really puts out the firepower!"

The Marine had not finished his last word when a green band of incoming automatic rifle fire walked up the dirt in front of him and licked the length of his silhouette from toes to head. The Marine made an indecipherable groan and fell back into the ditch on top of me. His last sound died on the fading wind, but a bad feeling gripped all the men in the pit of their guts. I pushed his body to the side and felt the hot, sticky pulsing of his blood as it spurted from the holes in his torso.

The whole team opened up with rifle fire into the tree line and the general vicinity of the Viet Cong's last position. We all knew the return fire was in vain, but we were angry about the death of our brother Marine. We slung his lifeless body between us. Holding him by the boots and his wrists, we hauled him back inside the perimeter. The lieutenant came up and received the sitrep from the team leader. Lieutenant Smith radioed Battalion at Phu Loc 6 that we had one Marine KIA (killed in action) and that we had been probed by a Viet Cong squad that had fired on our listening post. The one-man listening posts were secured for the night, but the fire-team-strength ambushes were left out in the field.

The following day was January 24, D day. Hotel would link up again with Foxtrot and begin the first day of Operation TUSCALOOSA. Charlie had a clear fix on our position and would be waiting to engage us somewhere along our river patrol route. No one got much sleep!

CHAPTER TWENTY-ONE

D Day—"The Refugees"

Just before dawn the ambush teams returned to the Hotel Company perimeter. The squad leaders were debriefed. Each squad reported seeing movement to its front and on its flanks. Marines reported hearing scuffling sounds in the fields to the front of the ambush teams' fighting holes. The Marines described sounds like crawling bodies scraping their weapons or web gear over rocky areas. However, since their orders were to fire only if fired upon, the ambushes had held their fire. The overall purpose of the ambushes was to provide early warning in case of an attack in force, at which time the teams would be withdrawn into the protective screen of Marine defensive fires. From time to time ambush-and-reconnaissance teams had been trapped outside the defensive perimeter of their units. When that happened it was "balls to the walls, and everyone fending for himself."

The Marines finished their morning pot of Joe and got into their flak jackets, helmets, and packs. Foxtrot filed through Hotel and led the long broken column toward the Song Thu Bon. Hotel followed in trace with Lieutenant Smith's Third Platoon on point.

The light battalion crossed several paddy clusters as the terrain descended into the river's floodplain. At 1200 hours on January 24, the lead squad from Foxtrot entered the hamlet of Bao An Tay, to which nineteen refugees had fled from the Viet Cong and North Vietnamese Army units to the east. During a routine search of the hamlet, Marines from Foxtrot's First Platoon uncovered several spider holes and bunkers inside huts, hidden under piles of rice and bamboo winnowing baskets. An M-14 rifle, several M-26 hand grenades, and a plastic-wrapped sheaf of documents were uncovered.

The company commander took a brief look at the documents and got on the radio to the Battalion Command Group at Phu Loc 6. "Crimson Leader, this is Crimson One-Six. Over."

The battalion radio operator monitoring the sweep and maneuver companies responded immediately: "Crimson One. This is Crimson Leader. Over."

"Crimson Leader. This is Crimson One. Advise Battalion Commander. Point squad of Crimson One found enemy documents vicinity of AT988527. Weapons and ammunition found in several bunkers in hamlet Bao An Tay. Nineteen refugees—repeat, nineteen refugees—collected fleeing from east in vicinity AT978530. Trench line found in vicinity of AT974528 containing enemy bunkers and possible enemy sapper units. Recommend air strike on AT988527—repeat, run air strike on AT988527. Hamlet is now deserted. Request CH-46 resupply chopper to evacuate refugees and documents to An Hoa. Crimson One. Out."

"Crimson One. This is Crimson Leader Actual. Over." The battalion commander, Lieutenant Colonel Airheart, had taken the handset from the duty sergeant and spoke clearly into the radio.

"Crimson Leader Actual, this is Crimson One-Six. Over," the company commander of Foxtrot said, identifying himself to the battalion commander.

Colonel Airheart said he'd send a resupply chopper and an engineer team. Then he said, "An air strike was called on Button Crimson. Assume control on your visual ID on Button Gold. Repeat, you have one flight Phantoms armed HE contact and napalm. Assume control on your visual ID on Button Gold. Air strike leader will drop napalm to seal off target, then saturate with HE. Contact Phantom Provider One on Button Gold to set up strike. Crimson Actual. Out."

The colonel and his staff—radiomen and intelligence and operations officers—strode in full combat gear into the prop wash of the giant Marine CH-46 helicopter. The back ramp of the Sea Knight closed. The jet engines throttled into a high whine as triple blades bit into the air currents and Crimson Leader Actual rose into the sky over Phu Loc 6's sandbagged bunkers and machine gun emplacements. The steady *whump, whump, whuuump* of three-bladed props could be heard clearly over the Song Thu Bon valley.

CHAPTER TWENTY-TWO

D Day—"The Phantoms"

As the CO's Sea Knight cruised toward the blue ribbon of river cutting through the huge green and brown rectangles of rice fields, events were growing more intense on the ground.

The Phantom jets had roared in low over the hamlet of Bao An Tay. The company commander of Foxtrot Company had assumed control of the four F-4s as they powered across the rice fields fronting the hamlet. The squadron commander had easily identified the friendly Marine forces in their jungle utility uniforms clustered along the main village street. Captain Burgett had shot an azimuth on his compass and plotted a heading for the Phantom Provider Leader's bombing run.

The CO of Foxtrot felt certain the Phantom jockeys could obtain a visual on the trench line once they dove low to commence their run. Just in case, he gave the flight leader a one-thousand-meter window and compass heading to guide the sleek gray jets down onto their target.

The Phantoms sliced through the air five hundred meters to the front and two thousand meters to the left flank of the Marines. Heading one-niner-six would take the twin-engine bombers down an invisible chute directly over the enemy bunkers and trench line. The four jets flew in a strung-out column behind the flight leader, Phantom Provider Leader.

After their initial high-altitude pass over the target, the flight of Phantoms banked slowly, coming around to the south of the village to line up their bombing run. Phantom Provider Leader nosed his plane into a shallow dive from two thousand feet and slowed his descent. The thirty thousand pounds of ordnance each Phantom was capable of carrying made it more of a rocket-ship bombing platform than a nimble bird of prey. Indeed, the F-4's wasplike beak, protruding ahead of low raking delta wings separated by huge twin jet engines, made the Phantom both easily recognizable and feared by the enemy as the Marines' main close air support weapon. As the gray lancet of the fuselage of Phantom Provider Leader screamed past the kneeling troops of Foxtrot Company, a pair of black drums tumbled off the underside of the jet's wings.

When the black drums impacted, no immediate explosion was heard by the troops on the ground. Instead, the sky to the front of Foxtrot was filled with a broiling, billowing cloud of black, punctuated in the middle and on the edges by orange fire that grew in intensity as the black smoke rose into the sky. No sooner had Phantom Provider Leader climbed above the smoke and fire and banked hard to port than the second aircraft swooped to rid itself of the hellfire beneath its wings. Another sheet of flame followed by black smoke was left in the second Phantom's wake.

The mountain of fire rose high into the air, and each succeeding Phantom's napalm load added to the effect, until the entire trench line and bunker complex was engulfed in napalm's deadly embrace. Even underground, no enemy soldier in that trench complex would survive, because the nastiest trait of napalm's burning gelatin was that it consumed all available oxygen above and below the surface.

As the plumes of smoke rose over the trench line, a group of peasants rose from the ground and started streaming straight toward the Marines in the village. Apparently, the villagers had been hunkered down in underground bunkers located between the napalm strikes and the village containing the Marines of Foxtrot Company. Miraculously, the clouds of fire had not reached the trembling peasants, who ran and stumbled, crying, into the village and threw themselves on the mercy of the astonished Marines. After a count was made, there were another seventy-five refugees to add to the earlier total of nineteen. Off to the south, the muffled *whump, whump, whuump, whuuump* of a Sea Knight helicopter became audible.

Crimson Leader Actual, aboard the Sea Knight, looked at the massive cloud of black napalm smoke outside of the right window. Under the left fuselage of the giant chopper the milling, frightened peasants were hidden from the CO's view. The CO would have to sort that mess out later. As he often said, "There's a hell of a lot to running a rifle battalion besides chasing Charlie."

Disembarking from the Sea Knight, the CO was assaulted with requests. First and foremost came the question of the refugees and their disposition. This matter was further complicated by the fact that two of the women refugees had actually been Viet Cong nurses hoping to slip through the Marine sweep companies by intermingling with the villagers and refugees.

"Good afternoon, sir!" The greeting of the commander of Foxtrot Company was crisp and military for the field.

"Afternoon, Captain! What the hell do we have here?"

"Sir, my men have collected refugees all morning. The F-4s made one run with napalm; no HE was dropped, sir. The trench line was visible from the air, and Phantom Provider lit up the target with the first pass. We secured the HE run, and by the time the napalm was burning itself out, all these dinks—er, excuse me, sir. All these peasants here came out of a bunker complex between the target and this village. Frankly, I can't figure out how they survived! These two here with Corporal May are Viet Cong nurses who tried to slip through our position with the refugees. That old man over there blew the whistle on them. He said the Viet Cong come into their village and take their rice and their young men. He's sick of this bullshit, Colonel. He said he doesn't care if they kill him or not!"

As though on cue, the old man looked straight into the eyes of the battalion commander and said, *"Ke thu cua linh, ke thu cua linh! Beaucoup Viet Cong linh. Di di mau, di di mau!"* One long skinny arm shook as he spoke and pointed away toward the river, which ran along a mile distant from the village of Bao An Tay.

"What in Hades is that old whitebeard babbling about?" the CO asked no one in particular.

"Sir, the Kit Carson Scout says the old man has been saying, 'Many Viet Cong soldiers, enemy soldiers run off toward the river,' sir." The captain had been privy to all the interrogations of the refugees that morning.

"Well, Captain, get these people on the chopper back to An Hoa. The ARVN interrogation teams can get the facts straight. Tell the old man thank you. We'll find Charlie down along the river. The question is will he come out to fight? Captain Burgett, I want Foxtrot and Hotel to link up in tight perimeters tonight. Send out ambush teams and LPs, and I want a fifty percent alert until oh-four-hundred hours. Carry on." The colonel glanced long and hard across the fields and paddies toward the river. "That's where we'll look for Charlie tomorrow, along the river. Good evening, Captain."

"Yes, sir. Good evening, sir!"

CHAPTER TWENTY-THREE

D Day—"Night Perimeter"

After Colonel Airheart had given Foxtrot's CO his orders, Captain Burgett called his platoon commanders and staff NCOs together.

"The colonel has ordered fifty percent alert for tonight. I want the fighting holes dug no farther than twenty-five meters apart. Emplace an M-60 machine gun every third bunker, and I want the platoon sergeants to personally inspect aiming stakes and interlocking fields of fire for each machine gun. I want one fire team out on ambush from each platoon. Emplace the fire teams half a klick to our front, spread out in a crescent with the flanking teams bending in on our perimeter. If attacked in force, the flanks will retreat into our perimeter and pull the center ambush team in as they fall back. If our ambush teams are tucked inside half a klick, there is no reason to field the listening posts. I will square that away with the CO. I want two of the teams to have PRC-10 radios, giving quarter-hour sitreps verbally or by breaking squelch.

"Gentlemen, we have a plan. I want absolute alertness

tonight! Charlie is out there watching us, and he could attack without warning. Thank you, gentlemen. Return to your platoons and carry on!"

The lieutenants and platoon sergeants then called their squad leaders together, designated the ambush teams, and defined the boundaries of the fighting holes making up the company perimeter. Hotel Company had received the same orders for its interlocking defensive ring of bunkers.

Lieutenant Smith strode among the Marines of Third Platoon and called the squad leaders up to explain the defensive perimeter orders given by the battalion commander. "Luther, I want Lafley's team out on ambush a half klick to our front. Lafley will move out at dark and link up with Second Platoon's ambush team. You will stay within sight of each other and carry a PRC-10 radio and give quarter-hour sitreps."

Hamilton knew that Lafley's team had been chosen because it was the saltiest in the platoon, and after the one-sided ambush on the river everyone knew it was the most sanguine.

"Luther, are we supposed to squelch the radio every fifteen minutes unless something unusual happens and we report verbal?" Lafley asked, wanting to make certain the radio procedure was clear, because no one on an LP or ambush wanted the perimeter guards to open fire if they were still out or were pulling back after sighting an enemy main body.

"That's right, Lafley. Squelch every fifteen minutes. Two clicks for 'situation clear' and continuous clicks for 'enemy in sight.' If you sight the enemy and can pull back, the lieutenant or his radio operator will acknowledge your clicks with three clicks, a pause, and three clicks. The platoon will hold their fire, and you men get your sorry butts back in pronto. Got it?" Luther always managed to make Lafley remember he was still only a team leader.

"Got it, Exalted Leader Luther! By the way, if any of the assholes on lines busts a cap at my butt coming in, he better not miss, 'cause I will terminate his offensive ass with extreme prejudice! Hey, Burns! How did Double-oh Seven terminate those maggots in *Goldfinger*, man?"

Burns, always the wiseass, played the dummy to Lafley's every question. "Extreme prejudice, man. That is secret agent lingo for 'blew their balls off, man!' " Burns and Lafley both started laughing. They just broke each other up.

"Lord Almighty, I have no idea how I'll get any sleep with you two shitheads on ambush. You better cut out the bullshit before your team goes out tonight, or *Charlie* will terminate your asses with 'extreme prejudice.' " Luther put up with Lafley and Burns because they were professional and very deadly.

Lafley's mood grew serious. "Get your gear checked and be ready to move out to the ambush site in thirty minutes."

The ambush teams grabbed their rifles and six magazines per man. They donned flak jackets and helmets, but did not wear their haversacks or carry any additional gear except a PRC-10 radio. Lafley led his team forward until they found a deep undulation in the downward-sloping terrain. The night had grown deep indigo with tinges of purple at the horizon. Except for crickets chirping in the brush alongside a large paddy farther toward the river, the silence was intense. Lafley glanced into the gloom toward the area where the next ambush team should be emplacing itself. After a few moments his vision cleared, and his eyes adjusted to the dim light that revealed the movements of the nearby team of Marines.

The hours passed, and Lafley's team kept "tuned in to their immediate front," but the intensity was ebbing. Then sounds of scraping wood or metal drifted toward the team from somewhere across a field to their oblique front.

"Wake up, man! Wake the fuck up!" PFC Burns whispered urgently between his teeth. He gripped his weapon, instinctively clicking the safety device off.

"What ya got, Burns?" Lafley said in a muted whisper.

"I think Charlie is runnin' that cattle trick that they pulled on Culbertson when they busted his ass on that LP last night," Burns said.

"No problem. Let the fuckers get into range and we'll cut their asses up before they can say Jim Dandy. All hands will open fire on Burns's first volley. Clear!" Lafley had hunted since childhood in Montana, and if he knew about anything it was letting the prey fall into the trap before pulling the trigger.

The bells on the animals clanged—*gong, gong, goong, gooong*—as the hooves impacted the dirt directly to the ambush team's front.

"Now!" Burns screamed as he fired a half dozen rapid-fire rounds directly into the silhouettes that stood motionless fifty yards to his front. The rest of the team opened up, and for fifteen seconds the reports of the rifles were deafening.

"Cease fire, cease fire, you crazy bastards!" Lafley yelled over the sound of gunfire. The last rifle barked and came down off the shooter's shoulder. The breathing was audible as each man waited for the enemy to return fire. No flashes or reports were heard in the paddy. Each Marine looked in wonder at his neighbor.

"What the hell is out there, man? I know I hit that son of a bitch with the first shots I fired. There ain't nothin' standin' out there. Is there?" PFC Burns was certain his initial volley had impacted the side of the huge cow that had filled his sights broadside. He had figured that the subsequent fires would have cut into any Viet Cong troops hiding behind the huge beasts.

"We got to go investigate the target. Culbertson, get your butt out there and check those cows. If you are fired upon, hit the deck and lay still. We'll fire over-head while you crawl back in. Got it? Okay, go man!" Lafley ordered.

I ran in as low a crouch as I could manage straight into the field to our front. The carcasses of three huge water buffaloes lay on their sides, neither moving nor making any noise. Great pools of sticky blood oozed down their sides and frothed at their gaping mouths. The animals had been shot to pieces. I noticed that the hind legs had been blown completely off the middle animal. I had seen enough. Just then the wind changed directions and brought the stench of congealing blood and certain death to my nostrils. While leaning on my rifle to keep from falling, I kneeled and threw up what little I still had in my stomach into the dirt furrows of the pasture. In a moment, I was on my feet and moving drunkenly back toward the ambush position.

Burns was the first to greet me as I slipped into the team's fighting hole. "What the hell's wrong with you, man?" he asked. The taste of stomach bile was still so sharp in my mouth that I couldn't speak. I just stared out into the pasture and held my aching guts with both arms. Visions of the wide-eyed, blood-splattered faces of the animals haunted me as I fought for control.

"Charlie wasn't out there, Burns, you dumb-assed cracker!" I shouted, finally able to put some words behind my thoughts. "Those water buffaloes must have broken out of their corral. There aren't any dinks out there whatsoever. We shot those pitiful animals to pieces. I'm not proud of that shit. I cannot condone killing animals, or women and children. This killing is getting out of hand, Lafley."

I was permitted my moment of righteous indignation by all present. Then Lafley spoke.

"Culbertson is grossed out about a couple of fuckin' water bo's!" he said. "Great, Culbertson, you can request mast tomorrow and tell the skipper how Lafley and Burns fucked up and capped some innocent water buffaloes that failed to recognize there's a war goin' on here. I personally do not give a shit what you like, Culbertson. We are here to kill Communist soldiers, and if a few water buffaloes get killed in the process that's just tough shit. Tell Culbertson about the Force Recon dudes we found up on the Z [DMZ], Burns."

"One afternoon, me and Lafley and Blocker were checking out the entrance to a deserted village," Burns said. "We entered the ville and couldn't find nothin' or nobody in the huts. Finally, Blocker walks over to a water well to fill up our canteens, and right there in a clump of bamboo trees they all are. Five Marines, man! A whole Force Recon team nailed to those bamboo trees with their peckers cut off and big old pieces of hide cut out of their chests. The North Vietnamese regulars caught the Recon dudes. Tortured the living shit out of 'em. Nailed 'em to the bamboo and started carvin' 'em up. I don't give a fuck what happens to Charlie or his water buffaloes! Those men they killed up on the Z were Americans. They were my brother Marines, and I want some payback from these little slant-eyed bastards." In twenty seconds, Burns expressed an anger that smoldered in most, if not all, of the veteran combat Marines I had met in Vietnam. They had all seen so much pain, horror, and death that they had become numbed psychologically to others' misery and pain, as well as to the recognition of their own. Burns wasn't an animal or monster; he was not interested in how he went about settling old scores—he just wanted them settled.

Sunrise broke over the fields leading toward the Song Thu Bon. Lafley's team grabbed their rifles and prepared to march the half a klick back to the Hotel perimeter. I sat looking at the corpses of the three huge buffaloes in the pasture. The blood that ran down the animals' swollen rib cages had turned almost black. Swarms of flies buzzed onto the carcasses, fighting for what nourishment they could steal from the once-proud animals. The eyes of the closest buffalo were protruding like giant ostrich eggs, with only the whites staring into the heavens. The animal's tongue lolled out slack at the jaw, as though the effort of wiping away all that blood had become just too much. A sadness coursed through my mind as I turned my back on the grisly scene and made my way to the company's lines.

CHAPTER TWENTY-FOUR

D Day Plus One—
"The Ambush"

At 0730 hours, Foxtrot assumed the battalion point and cut a trail along the paddies and dikes leading to the river. The information the old man had passed to the skipper of Foxtrot Company concerning "many Viet Cong soldiers running toward the river" would be checked out. Hotel Company saddled up and joined the long procession of Marines weaving their way ever closer to Charlie's river sanctuary.

The sun was up and the landscape was bright and bursting with life even as death looked for prey on its dikes and trails. Third Platoon was still on point as Hotel Company followed Foxtrot over dikes and paths that cut sharply right and left every hundred meters or so. From above, marching ahead through the immense rice fields only to tack right or left, the column must have resembled a lightning bolt.

About noon the point scout glimpsed a blur of figures running from the edges of a long ditch at the far end of the paddy some four hundred meters to his front. The Foxtrot point man yelled back down the column, "Tell the lieutenant it looks like six dudes

155

trying to make it to the village in that far tree line. Request permission to fire."

The Marine next in column behind the point came up and squinted into the bright sunlight. "Those are dinks, all right. Look, you can see those first two carrying rifles low and parallel to the ground. Let's take 'em down!"

The word took only a moment to come up to the point from Foxtrot: "Skipper says kill them if they are armed. Make positive ID and fire on point scout's command."

The point always called the shots once the CO authorized a volley; the point would fire on his own volition if the platoon was threatened or if he received incoming fire from hostile enemy positions. Once the point opened fire the rest of the troops picked up the firing discipline with an almost natural rhythm. The goal of the volley fire was to immediately achieve fire superiority and to suppress hostile fire. The power of volley fire was awesome. A Marine platoon was capable of interlocking fires so deadly that, even at five hundred meters, virtually nothing in their beaten zone would or could survive.

Foxtrot's point squad took up firing positions a couple of meters from the next man in a firing line that wound along the edge of the small mound where the point man had first sighted the enemy. The enemy soldiers continued to trot away from the Marines at a diagonal toward the protection of a village nearly two hundred meters distant.

The point scout spoke to the Marines on his port and starboard flanks. "Everybody got two-hundred-meter battle dope on their sights? Good, aim at the top of their heads the first few rounds. We ought to get torso hits. If the bullet strikes are in the dirt use Kentucky windage and hold a yard over the target. I got twenty bucks says I kill the lead dude by my third round. I got tracers; watch the bullets impact and then let's do some work on these assholes. Ready?" The point shouldered his M-14 rifle and held a twelve o'clock sight picture on the lead dink.

Whaaam! The first red tracer sped inches over the paddy and impacted in the dirt a foot in front of the Viet Cong's churning legs. *Whaaam!* The second tracer sliced along the same trajectory as the first bullet, but it inscribed a path a yard higher. The Viet Cong point man was knocked down hard to his side as the 7.62mm, 150-grain ball bullet broke his left shoulder and entered his chest, tearing out his lungs and heart. The Viet Cong was dead before he hit the dirt.

The point man was momentarily lost in the frozen image of the second bullet ripping into the running Viet Cong's body. Suddenly hundreds of rounds poured onto the remaining Viet Cong.

The *splang, splaang, whiing, whiiiing* of ricochets was distinct as bullets glanced off the trail and over and into the nearby village. There were no bodies left standing for the bullets to impact, and the point man called a halt to the sixty-second bloodletting.

"Cease fire, cease fire, you fucking maniacs. Jeez Louise, there ain't nothin' standing. Do any of you psychos see anything standing out there? Ease up, man!" With that announcement, all hands rose from their firing positions and the point broke trail toward the gooks who lay on the far edge of the paddy.

"It wasn't fair. We didn't give 'em a chance to get close to the village or nothin'. Shame on you, Marines!" someone in the rear of First Squad yelled up to the point. And everyone was so high on adrenaline that the laughing turned into hysteria and the point scout stopped the column and knelt down until the lieutenant restored order in the ranks.

"What the shit is going on up there?" the lieutenant yelled. "Point, move out! The captain is really pissed that the column is stopped in the middle of this paddy. Have you men lost your minds?"

In a matter of minutes the point squad of Foxtrot Company had reached the killing zone. The Viet Cong soldiers lay twisted like in a heap, with arms and legs headed in no particular direction. Beneath each of the six men was a growing pool of darkening blood. As First Squad flipped the corpses over onto their backs, the Marines realized the effect of their rifle fire.

"God Almighty, would you look at the chunks of meat tore out of those suckers!" the first rifleman exclaimed to anyone within earshot.

"There must be twenty holes in this one, man. He didn't even know what the fuck hit him!" the point scout said, offering his assessment.

"Look at this dude over here. He caught a couple of rounds in the face! Except now he ain't got a face." The automatic rifleman held the corpse up with his arms under the Viet Cong's armpits, and he clutched him so they seemed to waltz cheek to cheek. "Hey, man, look—this man asked me to dance and I accepted, but on closer inspection I have to survey [retire as unfit for service] his ragged ass, because he got all his damn teeth shot out."

That comment brought peals of laughter from the Marines now congregated around the corpses. Deep in the pit of my stomach something tightened. Charlie had to be watching, and Foxtrot's and Hotel's Marines had better not grow lax and let down their guard.

CHAPTER TWENTY-FIVE

D Day Plus One— "The VC Village"

After the column returned to a semblance of battle order, the point squad of Foxtrot split off to the east and closer to the river, while Hotel filed past the shot-up bodies of the VC squad. Marines in Hotel's First Squad retrieved an M-14 rifle that had been overlooked in a shallow canal ten meters from the enemy "trailer." Two M-26 hand grenades were also recovered close by one of the corpses in some thick grasses at the canal's edge. All the VC troopers had had packs, which were searched with no beneficial results other than convincing proof that the enemy soldiers were well armed and equipped with complete uniforms, extra rations, and ammunition. The dead men had been main force Viet Cong soldiers and not the guerrillas that often harassed Marine patrols in this area.

The column broke across a dike system leading into the village. We mistakenly assumed that the village, a hundred meters to our east, was not a hostile Viet Cong-controlled village that housed and fed a main force Viet Cong rifle platoon. Now that the Viet Cong squad had been wiped out, we didn't suspect an enemy threat of any sort. We were relaxed and loose as the village came into clear focus.

The first scattered burst of automatic AK-47 rifle fire shocked the point fire team out of its complacency and into action. Hitting the deck, the five Marines at the front of the column brought their rifle fire to bear on the first two huts in a long row of grass-roofed shacks that lined the main street of the village. The enemy rifle fire had spread out through the point team, with most of the bullets passing harmlessly overhead. However, one bullet had knocked the last fire team member onto his back, where he lay speechless with glazed eyes. The bullet had impacted under the Marine's right eye and passed through the cheekbone and jawbone, exiting underneath the right mandible and leaving a reddish burn channeling along the upper right side of his neck.

"Hey, man, can you talk? What happened? No one heard you cry out or anything!" The point scout and the rest of First Squad had gathered around the downed Marine in a protective perimeter with rifles facing the village. The rifleman who was hit just stared into the sky with a weird, dazed look on his face.

The lieutenant came up with his radio operator and looked down at the wounded man, one of the new replacements who had joined Hotel just before the operation kicked off. No one in the point squad even knew his name.

The lieutenant addressed the Marine, whose name finally had been proffered by someone as PFC Jones. "Son, are you hurting badly?" The lieutenant didn't know where to begin. Jones looked peaceful as hell, with only a black hole in his cheek and a trickle of blood running down his neck.

"I feel sleepy, sir. I don't hurt anywhere, sir. I just feel warm all over my face and neck, sir."

The lieutenant yelled down the column, "Get a corpsman up here on the double!"

The corpsman, a chubby black sailor carrying a large canvas medical bag and an M-14 rifle, but otherwise clad just like the rest of the grunts, came up and kneeled next to PFC Jones. The corpsman felt Jones's pulse and, tilting his head forward, shined a pin light into his eyes. The corpsman pressed lightly around the bullet's entry hole with his fingers, then, turning PFC Jones's head slightly, examined the exit hole in his neck.

"Lieutenant, this man doesn't appear to be in danger, and his pulse isn't greatly reduced. I think the bullet must have severed the facial nerves in the front of his face, sir. He's in mild shock now, that's why he feels warm. He's hemorrhaging inside his jaw area and needs to be medevacked as soon as possible, sir."

Lieutenant Smith looked toward the momentarily forgotten village, just a hundred meters to our oblique front. "Give me the handset, PFC Holloway. Luther, take your squad and form a firing line facing that village. If you see any movement, open fire. Is that clear?"

Protected by the berm of the shallow canal, Hamilton's men were already moving on line and taking up firing positions. "Aye, aye, sir! Do we hold position if fired upon, or do we assault the village, sir?"

"You and your men hold the line here. I'm calling in some artillery prep before we move into that village. Better safe than sorry, eh, Hamilton!" Lieutenant Smith was proving to be no dummy, and the Marines hustled to show him their approval.

"Yes, sir! We got this firing lane secured, sir. If Charlie sticks his fool head out of that village, he's history, sir!" Hamilton liked the platoon commander and would fight like "a hundred hells" to protect the lieutenant and the wounded Marine.

The lieutenant did not answer Hamilton, because the radio suddenly squelched to life. The lieutenant broke down the map coordinates and defined the weapons and the type of fire mission he wanted: "Steel Curtain, this is Hotel Point Leader. Enemy troops sighted in village vicinity of AT016539. Engaged in firefight. Six enemy KIA confirmed. Received incoming sniper fire from village. One Marine WIA. Request medevac, my position in rice paddy southwest of village one hundred fifty meters. Will show chopper yellow smoke. Over."

"Hotel Point Leader, this is Steel Curtain. I have your Six vicinity of AT016539, southwest of village in rice field. One casualty WIA requiring medevac. The medevac operations officer will be contacted to dispatch a Sikorsky UH-34 chopper. Over."

The artillery radio operator relayed the medevac mission immediately on the battalion's secure net and came back on the "hook" requesting the platoon commander's artillery schedule.

"Hotel Point Leader, this is Steel Curtain. Medevac is on the way. Give me your firing orders. Over."

"Steel Curtain, this is Hotel Point Leader. We are one hundred fifty meters southwest of village. We have no cover in this position. Give me a single Willy Peter [white phosphorus shell]. Coordinates are AT016539. Hotel Point Leader will adjust. Prefer 155 Mike Mike if available. Repeat, 155 Mike Mike, Willy Peter fire AT016539. Hotel Point Leader will adjust. Hotel Point Leader over." The lieutenant had at first thought about firing a smoke round from one of the 155mm howitzers in the four-gun battery back at the Eleventh Marines Fire Support Base at An Hoa. The smoke could drift and cover the Marine position in the rice field and allow Charlie an opportunity to attack.

"Hotel Point Leader, this is Steel Curtain. Fire mission. One round Willy Peter, 155 Mike Mike firing location AT016539. Hotel Leader will adjust. Over."

"Steel Curtain, this is Hotel Point Leader. Commence firing. Will adjust. Over." The lieutenant listened for the report of the single big gun back at An Hoa, the present command post in the rear.

A faint *kaboooom* echoed over the rice paddies. The huge 155mm shell was speeding into the skies in its upward trajectory, soon to turn downward. Thirty seconds passed and then the clouds were punctured by the screaming round plunging ever closer to the village. The shell slammed into the rice paddy at the village entrance only a hundred meters from the Marine position. The white phosphorus shell burst, sending bright burning stars of phosphorus in all directions from the impact point and high into the air. The burning shards of phosphorus made graceful white smoke trails as they arced upward.

The lieutenant was back on the net before the burning fragments had returned to earth. "Steel Curtain, this is Hotel Point Leader. Adjust fire, add one hundred meters. Repeat. Add one hundred meters, 155 Mike Mike, Willy Peter, fire for effect. Repeat. Willy Peter, fire for effect. Over."

The radio operator at Fire Support thought he had heard wrong—or that the young lieutenant, in his stressful situation, had mistakenly asked for more Willy Peter, instead of the standard mission of HE (high-explosive) rounds.

"Hotel Point Leader, this is Steel Curtain. Ready for fire mission. Correction. Firing HE, not Willy Peter. Repeat. Steal Curtain firing for effect, 155 Mike Mike with HE and point-detonating fuses. Over."

"Steel Curtain, this is Hotel Point Leader. Negative your last. Target is enemy village. Fire mission, 155 Mike Mike with Willy Peter. Fire AT016539 for effect. Repeat on my authority to run second fire mission. Steel Curtain, we are burning enemy village to the ground before my troops assault. Hotel Point Leader out." The lieutenant had called for more white phosphorus; he felt the platoon was too vulnerable to enter the village unless the Willy Peter rounds had already burned and smoked the enemy soldiers into the Marines' gunfire or out the rear end of the village.

Hamilton ran back to the wounded trooper and Lieutenant Smith. "Sir, the medevac chopper has been sighted. Permission to pop yellow smoke, sir."

"Yeah, Luther, throw the smoke behind us in that flat pasture and help these men get PFC Jones into the chopper. Son, you'll be at the battalion aid station in ten minutes. Good luck! We'll drop in on you when we get back in off operation. Get him into the chopper. Now, men, let's move!"

As the Marines carried Jones by his arms and legs into the cargo bay of the UH-34, the corpsman tied an identification unit wound tag on the man's utility shirt. This was done in the event the Marine lost consciousness or died en route to Battalion. The Sikorsky lifted off and headed low over the rice fields to the southwest, toward An Hoa.

The chopper had been in the air about two or three minutes when the pilot radioed his location to Battalion for the notification of Steel Curtain that the air was clear to run the fire mission. The four 155mm howitzers boomed in sequence at the Eleventh Marines Fire Support Base, where each gun was emplaced in its own sandbagged revetment. The shells for each gun were cased in wooden crates spread out around the circle of sandbags protecting the gun. The howitzers rested on flat steel platforms that allowed the gunners to get a true level on the gun's sights. The rubber tires supporting the guns lifted off the firing platforms and the cradles bucked as the giant barrels slammed back down the carriages in recoil, disgorging the spent shell casings. The range for the "155 Mike Mike" was a maximum of 14,600 meters. Reaching Lieutenant Smith's platoon in the rice paddy outside the village was a cakewalk for the gunners and crew of the Eleventh Marines.

Four rounds screamed downward toward the village. The noise increased. We got down, covering our ears and trying to tuck our bodies deeper into our flak jackets.

The first shell impacted at the center of the small village. The other three rounds fell into the general vicinity of the first shell's crater, although no one could make out the actual impact points due to the horrendous smoke and fire spreading through the area.

Wham! Wham! Whaaam! Whaaaaaam! Four separate and distinct secondary explosions were detonated by the Willy Peter fire and the roof of a large hut was blown into the air, only to break apart into hundreds of pieces of smoldering thatch. As the flaming roof material fell through the air, black-and-white plumes of smoking debris etched oddly graceful trails across the hellish landscape.

The lieutenant was immediately back on the radio to end the fire mission. "Steel Curtain, this is Hotel Point Leader. Secure fire mission. Village destroyed and burning. Repeat. Secure fire mission. Good shooting, Steel Curtain. This is Hotel Point Leader. Out."

"Jeez, Luther, did anyone bring any marshmallows?" Lafley said. "That fuckin' village is cooking! I wonder what it's like to be in the Gook army and go through shit like that. Who knows, those dudes will probably desert and head for Cambodia."

Luther cut the merrymaking short. "Saddle up and move out around the burning village to the next paddy system near that far hill," he ordered. "Lieutenant Smith says the company will dig in a tight perimeter for the night. The enemy is nearby, and today's contact confirms that we are up against regular troops, not the local dickheads. Let's move out fast, Point; we've got a lot of work left before setting up for the night."

CHAPTER TWENTY-SIX

D Day Plus One—
"H and I Fires"

In an hour of humping, Third Platoon of Hotel Company reached the base of the jungle-covered hillside that separated the long stretch of rice fields from the river. A perimeter was staked out by the platoon sergeants that interlocked with the perimeters of the other two platoons in the company. Twenty minutes later Foxtrot showed up and tied their perimeter into Hotel's southeastern flank. The Marine strength, including those out on the ambushes, numbered just over four hundred.

Fighting holes, spread fifteen meters apart in a tight ellipse, were dug by each fire team. The relatively steep hillside was to the rear of the battalion. The slope of the hillside was considered too densely undergrown to allow the VC to silently sneak up on us. Even so, when the ambush teams went out, a two-man listening post was emplaced halfway up the hillside to give us warning about Viet Cong advancing from that direction.

The evening sky was growing purple as the setting sun peeked over the emerald hills and silver paddies of the Arizona. The Eleventh Marines fire support commander was on the line to the Foxtrot and Hotel commanders, snug in their night perimeters. "Foxtrot Actual, Hotel Actual, this is Steel Curtain Actual. Over."

The commanding officers of Foxtrot Company and Hotel Company broke into the radio net individually.

"Steel Curtain, this is Foxtrot Actual. Over."

"Steel Curtain, this is Hotel Actual. Over."

"Foxtrot Actual, Hotel Actual. This is Steel Curtain Actual. Stand by for H and I fire to commence your sector at twenty-two-hundred hours. Targets are AT9663, AT9853, AT9953, AT9765. We have four plotted fire missions at your disposal impacting in line from western flank at AT983533 across your front two hundred meters southwest in hundred-meter intervals. Company commanders may call these support missions on Button Safeguard One, Two, Three, Four. Button Safeguard One is the westernmost mission. Any questions, Foxtrot? Hotel? Any regular fire missions can be run on Foxtrot Guardian or Hotel Guardian standard fire direction net. This is Steel Curtain Actual. Out."

The Foxtrot and Hotel commanders confirmed the night's artillery missions in their sectors to the fire support commander. Four H and I fire missions would commence at 2200 hours.

The troops huddled in their dugouts against the night's growing chill. Fifty percent alert was the order of the day, and half the grunts in Foxtrot and Hotel studied the gloom that blanketed the dusky fields to their front.

Promptly at 2200 hours, the 155 Mike Mike battery gunners at An Hoa sent four high-explosive rounds spiraling into the darkness toward the river. The grunts on guard duty in the lines heard the shells whine high over their positions and impact into the road junction a klick farther northeast. The orange-yellow explosions were quickly engulfed by the darkness. The resonance of the explosions carried into the far hills.

Burns had been out on fifty perimeters during his tour in Vietnam. In roughly fifteen minutes another salvo would leave the muzzles of the 155 Mike Mikes at An Hoa and another flight of shells would arch out into the Arizona. If Charlie was caught on the move within ninety meters of the impact zone of those shells, nobody would have to tag and bag his ass because there wouldn't be anything left. The report of four guns sounded in the southwest toward An Hoa; four more shells headed our way. Burns checked his watch. It showed exactly 2215 hours. Burns yawned and pulled his flak jacket closer to his heavy frame. The gunners at Eleventh Marines Fire Direction would run harassment-and-interdiction missions until 2300 hours. Then they would add two hundred meters to the range and fire the mission over, hoping Charlie would cross an impact zone that had already been fired. This was going to be a long night! Burns closed his eyes and shivered. "We ain't going to see Charlie's ass out here. No, sir, not tonight, but tomorrow just might be interesting," he said to himself.

And so the watches went until 0400 hours, when the platoon began to stir. It was January 26, 1967.

Operation TUSCALOOSA was at D day plus two. A radio message had just arrived from the battalion actual in the field at Phu Loc 6. The message ordered Foxtrot and Hotel to break off the action and sweep back to Phu Loc 6 at 1800 hours if Charlie had not been engaged by then. The operation would be scrubbed as a failure, and the general staff would grow even more impatient to have us meet the Viet Cong in battle.

The platoon leader called the squad leaders of Third Platoon together. Over a steaming tin of coffee, Lieutenant Smith gave the day orders to his leaders: "Men, the skipper has radioed from Phu Loc 6 that Operation TUSCALOOSA will be terminated at eighteen hundred hours if Charlie's base camp is not discovered. We will take the point and search the hamlets along the river all day into the western region of Duc Duc Province. Let's be especially watchful and keep the men alert and spread out. That is all, carry on!"

CHAPTER TWENTY-SEVEN

D Day Plus Two— "The General Staff"

Luther Hamilton stood outside his fighting hole and drained the last drops of hot coffee from his canteen tin. The jungle was heavier to his front, near the river. The generally flat rice fields began to undulate into the foothills surrounding the Song Thu Bon. The Viet Cong had not attacked or probed in force last night. Luther suspected the Viet Cong wanted the Marines to feel a false sense of confidence that the Communist soldiers had broken contact and returned to mountain sanctuaries to fight another day.

"Men, I want everyone on one hundred percent alert at all times today. The danger is that Charlie is shadowing us, waiting to attack. Never underestimate the enemy! Saddle up, we're point squad today," Luther said.

"Well, I don't know about the rest of these dudes," Burns said, "but I am sorely in need of a good killin'. So let's rout out these Commie skunks and have a field day on their asses." Burns rarely changed his mood.

"Lafley, go ask the lieutenant if Matarazzi can bring

175

his gun team up on the point. We may need the firepower if we get jumped on today," Luther commanded.

Lafley returned with Matarazzi, Jessmore, and their M-60, which was perched on Mat's right shoulder, its black barrel raked forward. Mat and Jessmore wore bandoliers of linked 7.62mm machine gun cartridges. The troops were glad the gun team was up front, and the confidence level of the individual riflemen soared.

"Men," said Luther, "everyone should have six full magazines and two full bandoliers of extra ammunition. Check your water supplies; I want everyone to have two full canteens. M-79 man, check your 40 Mike Mike rounds. You should carry twenty-four rounds HE and six smoke. Every rifleman should have a one-hundred-round carton of M-60 linked gun ammo. If we get hit, pass the ammunition up to PFC Jessmore immediately. Carry hand grenades if you want, but not over two per man. The radio operator will carry four yellow smoke grenades and two red smoke grenades. Everyone should have a sharpened bayonet and two C ration meals in his haversack. We will be resupplied in the late afternoon before we head back to Phu Loc 6. Any questions?"

Lafley couldn't resist one last chance to impress Burns with his remarkable wit. "Luther, I think that list about covers it. Except Burns and me ate extra chow last night, and I was wondering who will be carrying the extra toilet tissue. I feel a giant movement coming on, Great Leader!"

Lafley had hit the mark. Burns howled, dropping to

his knees. "That's rich, Lafley. I always knew you was full of shit."

Luther had a patrol to run and was in no mood to trifle. "Both of you perverts get on the point, where I won't have to listen to your bullshit. God Almighty, I would dearly like to meet your mothers when we get back to the world. Tell me, you two, did your parents have any children that lived?"

That comment brought wails of laughter from the entire First Squad. Lafley and Burns hung their heads, trying vainly to come up with a fitting rejoinder.

The voice of Lieutenant Smith rang down the column to the point squad. "Lafley, get on the point. Luther, get your squad off their butts and make a trail for the river. It's oh-eight-hundred; let's move out, Marines!"

The First Squad filed out of the perimeter and took the narrow footpath that led around the base of the hillside and through stands of taller trees interspersed with thicker vegetation. The point squad saw no sign of enemy activity, although the trail had been disturbed by heavy foot traffic. Lafley and Burns led the squad and the rest of Third Platoon into sparse woods. Visibility shrank to twenty feet as tall trees and thick brush surrounded the diminished trail. Soon the lieutenant passed the word to halt the column fifty meters ahead, where the Marines were to kneel down with absolutely no conversation or unnecessary movement. The point marched steadily ahead, and then the bushes parted, revealing the wide river and a sandbar stretching from flank to flank two hundred meters to the front.

Lafley motioned, his left hand extended upward, for the Marines in the column to halt. He then slowly motioned—openhanded, with his palm downward—for the men to kneel down quietly.

The lieutenant and the captain came up to the point squad's position and surveyed the wide gorge cut by the Song Thu Bon. The river split into two channels with a giant beachlike sandbar dividing the streams. The nearest stream ran under the high bank on which Hotel's commanders were deciding strategy. The riverbank itself was fifteen meters high and dropped into the closer stream, which was twenty meters wide. The huge sandbar rose from the far side of the closer stream and ran fully five hundred meters to the second stream. The second stream was fifteen to twenty meters wide and looked to be similar to the closer stream, which ran a fast current directly under our position. Small dunes broke up the otherwise flat surface of the sandbar. Far to the port and starboard flanks the river's divergent streams joined.

The captain spoke to the Battalion Command Post at Phu Loc 6, reporting our location.

After much deliberation by the staff, platoon commanders were ordered to move their point squads into the river. After the crossing was made, they were to form up into skirmish lines and advance, taking advantage of available cover. Point squads were to halt two hundred meters from the opposite bank and, taking available cover, assume firing positions until artillery missions were run.

CHAPTER TWENTY-EIGHT

D Day Plus Two—
"River Crossing"

The squad leaders passed the word to the troops, who were growing tired of waiting. Lieutenant Smith and the company commander had come forward to ensure that the orders governing the crossing were understood clearly.

The lieutenant emphasized, "Men, after the first stream is crossed, form into a skirmish line and get some space between you. Advance on the far stream, halting at least two hundred meters from the far bank. Under no circumstances are you to cross the second stream until ordered to do so. If we take any hostile fire, we will be firing an artillery mission and perhaps an air strike. If fired upon, you may return fire at will. We will have 60 Mike Mike mortars emplaced in the rear of your position to provide overhead support if we get hit. PFC Culbertson will take the point, followed by Lafley and Burns. Hamilton, watch your distances carefully and seek all available cover. Captain, do you have anything to add, sir?"

The company commander looked over the men of First Squad carefully. "Any questions, men?"

I spoke up, since I had to take the point. "Sir, if there are enemy troops on that far bank, how come we don't fire some artillery prep before we get stuck down on that sandbar?" I thought it was a reasonable question, since there wasn't a damn thing on that sandbar to protect us if Charlie was on the far bank.

"Private, you came to Vietnam to kill Charlie, didn't you?" the captain said slowly. "We all came over here for the same reason, but you have your job and I have mine. Your job is to get in that river and set up on that sandbar. Mine is to worry about the artillery and the enemy if they are over there. Now, men, we are a team. Let's remember we're Marines. No one finer! If Charlie is over there, we'll massacre his ass. Now, let's get across that stream. Good luck, Marines!"

There was nothing we could say. The captain was a fine salesman, and in past engagements he had been "Johnny on the Spot" with the artillery fire missions. We just hoped that the lieutenant and the captain had their act together that day. We all felt we were going to need a steady hand and a clear head at the controls.

As I passed through First Squad, Luther Hamilton had a last word of advice. "Keep your rifle above the water line crossing the river. Let's go get after Charlie's butt," he said. I picked my way down the dirt path that was overgrown with the roots of trees lining the riverbank. The trail turned back on itself halfway down the bank, so I entered the first stream facing downriver toward Foxtrot. I could make out the splashes of Marines in midstream a klick to my left flank. As the Marines plodded in slow motion through the chest-deep water, the point of Foxtrot's lead squad seemed to fight the river current. I reached the end of the bank and stepped off into the stream. The water was shockingly cold! I got a good footing and, M-14 raised above my helmet to keep the weapon dry and aid my balance, began to ford. I moved with great effort out into the water's turbulence, and felt the constant tug as the current pushed against my legs and torso. My attention was focused solely on gaining ground ahead while keeping upright, when several bullets cracked over my head.

Small geysers of water splashed my face as the bullets tore by. The Viet Cong snipers on my left flank had opened fire between Hotel and Foxtrot from our side of the riverbank, or perhaps some of the fire was coming from my right flank as well. We were trained to continue moving through flanking fire. The only danger in facing flanking fire is to freeze in the beaten zone, where the incoming bullets impact. If the impact area is crossed by marching ahead through the fire, then the individual is exposed only for the time he bisects the kill zone. Most of my body was protected by the water, so I just struggled harder against the current's pull until I reached the far bank. But driving my legs in waterlogged boots and soaked jungle utilities took its toll my stamina. I lay exhausted against a five-foot-high sand dune that had to be negotiated to reach the flat stretches of the "island sandbar."

Lieutenant Smith had observed the progress of First Squad, as his Marines struggled against a four-foot-deep channel of fast, twisting current.

"Captain," he said, "the river was supposed to be at

low levels and be easily navigable on foot. Sir, the men look exhausted after the crossing, and the sniper fire is increasing from both flanks. Request sitrep transmission to Battalion to stand by with the fire support missions, sir."

The captain nodded and the company radio operator gave him the handset.

I stabbed the butt of my M-14 deep into the sandbank obstacle that I had to climb to get even footing on the sandbar. My boots dug into the wet sand as I struggled up terrain that slipped away under my feet. It seemed impossible to make any upward headway in the shifting sand, but a dozen bullets cracking over my head urged me over the top.

I lay on my side, wiping the wet sand off my weapon, and gazed back at the rest of First Squad as the men strained at midstream to conquer the steady drag of the current. I rose to my knees as Lafley and Burns lifted their bodies over the sand dune by leveraging their weight on their rifle butts, then fell onto the sandbar next to me. The incoming rifle fire had grown more intense, and we crawled apart to await the rest of the squad. Finally, First Squad was assembled and crawled forward to the point designated by Hamilton. We removed the 60 Mike Mike mortar rounds from one another's haversacks and stacked them in a loose pile for the mortar team that followed.

Grabbing our rifles, our main sources of protection, we moved ahead, with me on the point, for a distance of two hundred meters. The second stream came into view clearly a hundred and fifty meters to our front, where it flowed along the red earth of the southern bank. The sandbar was etched with gullies and defilades where the rains had cut shallow channels across it. From the place where First Squad had entered the river, the sandbar stretched three hundred meters away to the second stream. The surface of the bar had appeared very flat from fifty feet above; the real topography of the sandbar was small dunes and clumps of grasses across the undulating sand.

In roughly the middle of the sandbar island, First Squad got down in the most protected depressions afforded by the sand dunes. I pulled a bale of reed-bound twigs over on its side and knelt behind it. Realizing that most of my body was unprotected by the reed bundle, I fell to a prone position at the side of the reeds and began to push the sand under my body out and away from me. In a few short minutes, I had created a shallow hole hiding 50 percent of my body from enemy fire.

The captain observed First Squad's progress from the northern bank and made his second report to Battalion. The Hotel commander reported that the point squad had moved across the sandbar two hundred meters from the southern bank. The point squad was holding position in firing line awaiting an artillery fire mission. He also reported that the squad had received one hundred rounds of enemy sniper fire and sporadic fire from the far riverbank.

Individual shots rang out on the far bank. It appeared that enemy troops were manning the positions to First

Squad's front and were pouring increasingly heavier rifle fire onto the Marine lines. Second Squad had crossed the first stream and was moving across the sandbar in skirmish line behind First Squad.

Shots punctuated the air close over the bodies of First Squad. The sniper fire from our flanks was no longer audible, as First Squad was a couple of hundred meters farther up the sandbar island past the impact zone in the first stream.

Lafley yelled at Burns in the first moment after the enemy opened fire from high on the southern riverbank. "Burns," he said, "this shit is close, man. We can't maneuver on this sandbar. I say just keep down and we'll be all right. Captain will call in the artillery soon."

"Jeez, man, I hope so," Burns replied. "This stuff is right on top of me. I can't move a muscle. Where the fuck is Culbertson?"

I yelled back at Burns, "Hey, Burns, I fired a couple rounds and my rifle jammed. Bolt won't chamber another round. What the hell do I do now?"

Burns was quick to answer as the rounds sang through the air and kicked up sand in our faces. "Put your weapon down, dumbshit! If it don't work, forget it. Keep your fucking head down and you'll make out!"

As Burns's words reached my ears, a bullet slapped into the forearm of my rifle stock, sending splinters into my face and eyes. Another round cut the canteen off my butt. More rounds cracked through the air as the enemy fire picked up a rhythm. A chilling scream was emitted by someone to my right.

"Ahhaaaah! Ahaaaaah! I'm hit! Dammit, I'm shot in the face! Someone, please help me. I'm shot in the face!" After making a series of low moans and whimpers, the wounded Marine fell silent. Several Marines crawled to the downed man, who was dead when they got to him.

"Luther, it's Rivers. He's taken a burst in the face. He's dead, man. Jesus, where is that fucking artillery?" the voice of Jessmore sounded from my port flank. He sounded weak and distant.

"Jessmore, you can't help him now, man. If he's dead get away from him and stay down. The artillery will be here soon," said Hamilton, his voice quivering. We all knew the artillery would not be there soon enough.

The enemy firing picked up pace and the *crack, crack, crack, craacckk* of the AK-47s was joined by a heavier, richer resonance as the Viet Cong wheeled a 12.7mm heavy machine gun into position and began hammering us. The Viet Cong also began to lob 82mm mortar rounds high over our position onto the sandbar. The impacting rounds crunched into the sand as the shells were walked into our platoon's firing lines and back out the rear.

Mortar rounds quickly began to fall around us, their detonations sending geysers of sand into the air. A round hit ten yards from me, and the explosion lifted my body off the deck, but the round penetrated so deeply into the sand that the shrapnel's bursting radius was greatly reduced.

More rifle fire and automatic weapon bursts slammed around us, as a steady *thump, thump, thump, thuump* joined the staccato ring of the incoming rounds. A violent scream echoed from the man in front of me, and my face was suddenly spattered with bloody flesh. A Marine stumbled to his feet amid the roar of incoming rounds. A bright red splotch covered his buttocks and tapered down the legs of his utility trousers as he staggered toward the enemy trench line high atop the far bank. He moaned as he walked, "Fucking bastards! Kill me, you fucking bastards!"

The Marine lurched to a halt and doubled over into a crouch before dropping to his knees. Another burst of fire had impacted his gut and taken his life. The Marine raised both hands like a preacher on Sunday morning and, groaning inaudibly, fell forward onto his face.

I scraped at my face and pieces of flesh saturated with the dead Marine's blood came off my cheeks into my palms. The first burst of automatic weapons fire that had hit the man had torn the tops of his buttocks off and flung them in my face. The Marine had then jumped to his feet and staggered forward, only to get hit again in the midsection and bleed out as he hit the ground facedown.

Then the truth hit me like an icy shower. We were pinned down and in the proverbial "world of shit" that each of us always feared might come to pass. I concentrated on staying alive by keeping low, since my weapon would not function. And since everyone who had so far exposed himself had been shot, it was not a good time to go out and retrieve a weapon from my fallen comrades.

* * *

The company commander had put the first two platoons on the sandbar, and glancing from port to starboard along the firing line of Marines, he knew for certain that Charlie had engaged completely. "Give me the handset!" The captain was anxious to report to Battalion that the enemy had taken the bait—those of us on the sandbar—and was pouring over five hundred rounds per minute onto the positions of Hotel Company.

"Crimson Leader Actual, this is Crimson Two Actual. Over." The Colonel held the mike in a steely grip back at Phu Loc 6. "Crimson Two, this is Crimson Leader. Go."

"Crimson Leader, this is Crimson Two. Achieved lockup. Platoons One and Two now heavily engaged. Estimate one company main force Viet Cong. Firing AKs, AWs, heavy MGs, 82 Mike Mike. Estimate enemy strength at two hundred in trench line fifteen hundred meters long running west to east in grid squares AT9552 and AT9652 along main road. Casualties estimated at this time as seven USMC WIA. Request medevac after artillery mission run. Request fire mission—155 Mike Mike and eight-inch guns fire Willy Peter on trench line at AT955534 south. Repeat, south bank of Song Thu Bon. Over."

"Crimson Two Actual, this is Crimson Leader Actual. Medevac will have to wait until sandbar is cleared. No LZ is available for Marines under fire until enemy position is assaulted. Fire mission is being run on AT9552 and AT9652. Firing 155 Mike Mike with Willy Peter. Crimson Two Actual will adjust. Over."

The colonel knew the wounded Marines on the bar could not be reached until Charlie was rousted out of his defensive trench line on top of the southern riverbank. To move Charlie out required artillery prep fires, which the company commander could adjust from his vantage point on the northern bank. Once the artillery had Charlie reeling, the battalion commander would order the rifle platoons into the assault.

"Crimson Leader Actual, this is Crimson Two Actual. Expedite fire mission. Repeat, expedite fire mission. Troops under extremely heavy fire and mortar attack midsection of sandbar AT9972. Crimson Two Actual. Out."

The bullets splashed into the sand and whined over the worried souls of Third Platoon. PFC Holloway had screamed that he'd been shot in the head. The Marines that crawled to his position pulled off his helmet, which had a perfect bullet hole drilled in the front, two inches above the visor lip. The bullet had hit the inside headband bracket and deflected around the left of Holloway's helmet, blowing out his left eardrum and caroming out the rear of the steel pot into Holloway's pack, where it lodged harmlessly in his spare skivvy shorts. Holloway had the reputation of being the luckiest dude in Hotel Company. He always won all the large pots in five-card stud, and his luck had definitely held out this time.

I glanced to the rear as sand was kicked into my face. I couldn't believe my eyes! Lieutenant Smith was running forward through our position with his .45-caliber pistol in his hand. He was gesturing and waving the pistol, screaming like a madman: "Come on, Marines, follow me! Let's go, men. Follow me!"

The lieutenant had just passed my position heading toward the enemy trench line where the gut-shot Marine lay dead. The motion of Lieutenant Smith's churning boots arrested in mid-stride as a burst of AK automatic fire hit him in the chest. The bullets tore completely through Lieutenant Smith's flak jacket and out the back, and a dark circle spread out from the center of his back. The lieutenant's body shook as the bullets struck, and then he was hurled off his feet onto his back, where he lay senseless.

Hamilton yelled out clearly, so all his men could hear, "Stay down, you stupid bastards. I don't want no heroes here! Hold your positions and return fire. Corpsman! Corpsman! The lieutenant is hit! Get the fucking corpsman up here."

Back along the flattened Marines' firing lines the cry "Corpsman up!" was passed urgently along. Finally, a short, fat navy corpsman made his way through the sand dunes and knelt at the dead lieutenant's side. *Wham! Wham, whaam, whaam! Whaaam! whaaam!* The incoming rifle fire sought out the young medic as he leaned over to check the vital signs of a man he must have guessed was already dead. A hail of bullets cut the corpsman to pieces as he knelt silently, attempting to perform a miracle. His body fell over on top of Lieutenant Smith's.

Not realizing that both the lieutenant and the corpsman were already dead, the platoon sergeant from First Platoon ran to the lieutenant's side. The accurate fire of a dozen SKS rifles split the morning air, and the plunging fire sliced into the platoon sergeant. The first several rounds lanced through the sergeant's legs and twisted him in the air like a bass trying to throw a lure. The second volley slammed into his chest and face, and splattered the corpses on the deck with a fresh curtain of American blood.

Hamilton's voice cut through the rifle fire. "Dammit, I told you assholes to stay down. Now, stay down! We got artillery on the way, and we'll get off this fucking beach."

I heard the word *beach* and started to wonder what the hell Iwo Jima had been like. I decided that it could have been worse than this, but I didn't know how. I knew we had been pinned down in this exact position for over an hour already, and the sun said it wasn't near 1200 hours.

The Marines in the rear, near the north bank of the river, passed the word forward until it reached us in Third Platoon: "Get down, artillery is on the way!"

Thank God for that, I thought, and began a series of nonstop short prayers asking forgiveness for all the "wrong shit" I had done in my life. I then asked God to save me, because I promised I would find "constructive shit" to do later in life if allowed to live. The old saying that there are no atheists in a foxhole is a fact to which I will gladly testify.

Then the first artillery round from An Hoa spun down from the sky over our position and impacted in the stream to our front at the foot of the enemy riverbank.

The company commander was on the radio adjusting the fire.

"Steel Curtain, this is Crimson Two Actual. Over."

The FSCC (Fire Support Control Center) at An Hoa was "up" on the radio net. "Crimson Two Actual, this is Steel Curtain Control. Over."

"Steel Curtain, this is Crimson Two Actual. Adjusting fire mission 155 Mike Mike, Willy Peter, AT955534. Drop a hundred and fifty meters. Repeat, drop one-five-zero meters to AT955534, fire HE for effect. Repeat, fire HE for effect. Over." The Hotel skipper had shortened the range to the white phosphorus spotting round's impact and changed the type of warhead to high explosives.

"Crimson Two Actual, this is Steel Curtain. Fire mission. Fire 155 Mike Mike, HE, AT955534. Drop one-five-zero meters. Fire for effect. Fire support on the way. Steel Curtain. Out."

Every head on the "beach" was buried in the sand, but all ears strained heavenward in anticipation of the first salvo of "saintly intervention" fired from the howitzers at FSCC An Hoa. The four heavy rounds screamed their arrival and flung themselves in perfect order onto the enemy bank. The heavy rifle and machine gun fire that had been raking our dugouts in the middle of the sandbar stopped immediately. The enemy positions were hidden inside the black clouds of tumbling, roiling smoke that rose hazy against the dark verdant hues of the jungle foliage. Another fire mission was run after the first, and its shells impacted in roughly the same area, on top of the southern bank of the river. The Marines in Third Platoon could not assess the damage in terms of casualties wrought by the two fire missions. Incoming rifle fire had ceased, and we began to feel a degree of relief.

A rifleman to my left moved his position to afford himself more cover. But the Viet Cong soldiers had reentered the sawtooth of narrow trench line from the underground bunkers in which they had apparently weathered the artillery shelling without fatalities. Sand kicked high in the air and a long burst of enemy machine gun fire outlined the newly occupied fighting position. The Marine peered over the lip of his depression and the second volley of incoming small-arms fire cut him down. Suddenly he was motionless, on his back, his heart pumping ever-smaller rivulets of blood from the half dozen rents in his chest.

The captain was back on the net to FSCC An Hoa. "Steel Curtain, this is Crimson Two Actual. Over."

The radio came to life. "Crimson Two Actual, this is Steel Curtain Control. Over."

"Steel Curtain Control, this is Crimson Two Actual. Repeat fire mission, 155 Mike Mike, HE delayed fuses, AT9552 across AT9652. Target is road running west to east fifteen hundred meters along southern bank Song Thu Bon. Enemy has reentered trench line and is engaging friendly forces. Continue to fire for effect along trench line until Crimson Two Actual terminates mission. Over."

"Crimson Two Actual, this is Steel Curtain Control. Fire mission AT9552 across AT9652. Target is road running west to east fifteen hundred meters along southern bank Song Thu Bon. Fire 155 Mike Mike,

HE delayed fuses. Repeat, HE delayed fuses. Enemy is in trench line with bunkers engaging friendly forces. Fire for effect until Crimson Two Actual lifts the barrage. Crimson Two Actual, this is Steel Curtain Control. Running fire mission. Out."

The coordinates were already dialed into the four-howitzer battery at FSCC An Hoa. Delayed-action fuses were hurriedly chosen for the clusters of projectiles that stood silently by each gun. The delayed-action fuses would allow the shells to penetrate deep into their targets before detonating. This would result in underground explosions, which should reach the enemy soldiers as they waited out the artillery missions in their bunkers.

At My Loc 2, the two 105mm howitzers helilifted by Echo Company, Second Battalion, Eleventh Marines had been engaged since Foxtrot began crossing the single stream of the Song Thu Bon a thousand meters to the east of Hotel Company. Foxtrot had received several thousand rounds of incoming automatic weapons fire, rifle fire, and 82mm mortar fire from enemy soldiers dug into a trench line on the opposite bank of the river at their crossing point. The trench line actually ran for over two thousand meters to the west and met up with the trenches that opposed Hotel Company's assault at the objective on the southern bank of the Song Thu Bon's breaks.

Intelligence had been gathered from several wounded enemy soldiers captured on the previous day. What was initially believed to be a reinforced company of Viet Cong regulars and guerrillas was in fact the R-20th Viet Cong Main Force Battalion, led by a professional cadre of North Vietnamese officers and NCOs and supported by a number of guerrilla fighters. The enemy had shifted his forces up and down the riverbank through a series of trenches so as to disguise their numbers while lining up defensive fires to oppose Foxtrot's and Hotel's Marines as they attempted to cross the river. The river had been deeper and the current much swifter than Marine intelligence had estimated. These realities had slowed the Marine advances and afforded the enemy marksmen and mortar crews ample time to set up their attackers.

The artillery fire mission targeting Hotel's adversary in their bunkers had begun. Salvos of four rounds each impacted along the enemy trench line. Every minute a salvo slammed into the road and trench complex above the southern riverbank. Great heaps of dirt, wood, and vegetation lifted into the air as the lethal delayed-fuse shells dug into the earth and penetrated the heavy timbered bunkers before exploding. The enemy soldiers were torn to pieces as they huddled in the darkened silence of their dugouts that had become tombs.

After a steady twenty minutes of destruction, the Hotel's company commander got on the radio net to FSCC An Hoa. The 155mm howitzers grew silent.

CHAPTER TWENTY-NINE

D Day Plus Two—
"The Assault"

The moment the artillery fire was lifted, the Hotel skipper scanned the far bank and tree line with his binoculars. There was no sign of life! Craters had been torn into the sides of the riverbank and great tree trunks stabbed at unnatural angles into the air. The bank was littered with the twisted, broken bodies of dozens of enemy soldiers tossed from their bunkers as the powerful shells exploded. A gray-black haze hung like a veil of death over the enemy sanctuary. The captain ordered his remaining platoon commanders and NCOs to form an assault line and conduct a frontal assault on enemy positions.

"Crimson Two Actual, this is Crimson Two Blue Leader. Moving on line to conduct frontal assault through enemy position. Will advise when objective reached. Crimson Two Blue Leader. Out."

"Crimson Two Actual, this is Crimson Two Red Leader. Roger Blue Leader's command. Moving into assault line, Crimson Two Red Leader. Out."

"Crimson Two Actual, this is Crimson Two White Leader. Confirm Blue and Red Leader taking the point of assault line. Crimson Two White Leader will reinforce first wave. Crimson Two White Leader. Out."

The captain watched as the three rifle platoons deployed to begin the company assault on the southern bank's bunkers, whatever was left of them. Blue (First) and Red (Third) platoons would assault side by side, followed by White (Second) Platoon, which would mop up after the lead wave had swept through the enemy. The captain paused a brief moment and savored the sight of a hundred and fifty Marines forming up "on line" to assault a well-armed, professionally led, tenacious regular Viet Cong main force battalion. This was as close to the action at Iwo Jima as it was ever going to get in Vietnam. This was the real Marine Corps in action.

Down on the beach, First and Third Platoons heard the cry: "On line. The captain wants every Marine on line. First and Third platoons form the first assault line. Second Platoon will bring up the rear." The gunnery sergeant who had taken command of Third Platoon after Lieutenant Smith was killed shouted the command to the troops huddled in their shallow holes. The cries and screams of wounded Marines were everywhere. Shouts of "Corpsman up! Someone help me, please. I'm shot in the face. Blinded, please, someone help me!" went unanswered, as most Marines were already applying bandages and compresses to wounded buddies.

Men lay in every imaginable posture. Some were sitting with bloody bandages wound around their heads. One man lay with glazed eyes as others pressed a battle dressing over his gaping chest wound to stop the air from sucking in and drowning him in his own blood. One man staggered through the sand with still bodies strewn around him, laughing hysterically at his arm, held up in front of him, the hand blown off at the wrist. There was no time to estimate casualties at that point, and Foxtrot was having an equally hard time down the river at its crossing point.

The Marines who were still ambulatory staggered forward to form the assault line ordered by the company commander. Gunnery Sergeant Gutierrez gave the order to commence the assault. "Fix bayonets, men. On line, forward march! Commence firing." The grunts had formed a line about seventy men across. They marched ahead, M-14 rifles at the hip, firing on semiautomatic in the general direction of the trench line because being above the advancing Marines, the enemy position was not clearly visible from the level of the beach.

The remaining VC "suicide soldiers" took up firing positions and waited for the Marine assault line to get into range. Barely aware of the tangle of comrades that sprawled with lifeless limbs and gaping eyes in their very midst, they peered apprehensively over the lip of their defensive earthworks.

The assault reached the second stream and marched confidently into the chill current. The depth of the stream was not over two feet at midchannel, and the going was effortless compared with the first water obstacle. As the Marines reached midstream a fusillade of shots echoed from the bank as the Viet Cong fired a plunging volley into the line. Several Marines were hit, but only one man crumpled, to be left motionless in the river as the Marines drove their churning legs into the clay and tried to get enough traction to scale the south bank.

A squad of Viet Cong soldiers had remained in the enemy trench line to oppose the assaulting Marine company. They had been wounded badly enough for their commanders to be unwilling, or unable, to take them to the rear when the main body of the main force battalion's troops withdrew to the west toward the villages of La Bac 1 and 2.

The Second Platoon had assumed a firing line with twenty-five Marines and two M-60 machine guns positioned to shoot overhead in support of the first assault line. As the squad of Viet Cong in the trenches opened up on the lead platoons, Second Platoon's firing line strafed the top of the bank, chewing the top off the trench line. The red tracers of the M-60s lanced into the dirt fortifications of the enemy troops. Chunks of earth and wood were kicked high in the air by the bullets' grazing fire. The VC suicide squad had performed its mission. Its remaining members crouched low in their holes as the Marines' automatic weapons raked the ground inches above their heads.

First Squad, leaping over the top of the bank, was halted by the sight of a company of Viet Cong regulars sprawled in silent disarray. The dead had assumed postures that would be impossible for the living. Arms and legs were wrapped around necks and heads. Arms were reaching for a neighbor's leg that was missing at the knee. Limbs were poking out of loose mounds of earth, as though they were searching for lost bodies. One Marine felt a drop of hot liquid splash onto his face as he leaned against a ruptured tree trunk. He reached out his hand to wipe his face and more droplets fell onto his hand. The dull red liquid was thick and warm as soup. Looking around at the piles of dead Viet Cong, he could find no source for the droplets of blood. Then the Marine tilted his head upward, peering along the scarred tree trunk. From the crotch of the crippled tree, the bulging eyes of a dead Viet Cong soldier gaped down at the Marine. The dead soldier's body had been blown into the air and landed on the tree limb, head facing the ground ten feet below. The right side of his face and his right arm had been blown off. Congealing blood still ran down the gaping wound in his cheek onto his chin, where the droplets gathered until gravity caused them to fall, splattering the base of the tree. The Marine wiped the blood off his face with the back of his hand and stared at the ground at his feet. Flies were already clustered around the pool of blood that stretched away from his boots in all directions.

The dozen survivors of the trench line defenses were bayonetted by the Marines who crossed the banks. There was no more resistance. The Viet Cong soldiers who had earlier escaped to the main road were long gone. The troopers of First Platoon and Third Platoon advanced to the tree line fifty meters from the riverbank. A report was made to the company commander, who was moving his command post forward, by the Third Platoon leader: "The assault line penetrated enemy trench line. No enemy survivors. Awaiting orders. Over."

The company commander needed detailed

information before a situation report could be made to Battalion. The command posts at Phu Loc 6 and Da Nang wanted to hear the "numbers." The personal side of the engagement could wait.

"Crimson Two Red Leader, this is Crimson Two Actual. Request accurate body count of enemy dead. Repeat, accurate body count of enemy dead. Need estimated size of enemy unit surviving attack and direction of escape. Medevac choppers are on the way from An Hoa. Over."

The gunnery sergeant had been around the Corps long enough to know what information was required by Division for their reports to III MAF (Marine Amphibious Command) in Da Nang. He told his squad leaders to get a body count and double-check it.

From opposite ends, Burns and Lafley counted bodies in the trench. As Burns passed under the tree with the bloody Viet Cong soldier hanging out of the crotch, he called out, "Hey, Gunny, do we count fractions? This fucker here ain't got no arm and only half a face. I think I make that about three-quarters of a gook. Is that okay, Gunny?"

Gunnery Sergeant Gutierrez was in no mood for Burns's shit. "Burns," he yelled, "if you don't have that count in two minutes, I'm gonna make you sit here and guard these decaying bastards all day. You want that, you freckle-faced fat boy? Now, get me an accurate count for the skipper!"

Lafley was finished before Burns started to count again. "Gunny, I got fifty-seven KIA. I think most of 'em are by artillery. They're so fucked up I can't tell what the hell happened to 'em."

"Okay, Lafley, that's good. We got fifty-seven KIA. No WIA. How many friendly?"

Again Lafley spoke up. "Gunny, we got twelve Marines KIA and about forty-two WIA from rifle fire and mortars. We have two corpsmen KIA from rifle fire. That's approximate. The medevac chopper is coming into the beach now, Gunny."

Lafley gazed off the edge of the southern bank along the sandbar, which was littered with casualties. The giant Sea Knight hovered over the sand as though it was afraid to tarnish the sacred ground where so many Americans had fallen. The sandbar where the Marines had endured Charlie's continuous heavy fire for over two hours was a scene of utter confusion. Marines exited the huge cargo ramp of the chopper with a stretcher only to return carrying a wounded Marine. The wounded were collected hastily and tended to inside the chopper's cargo bay by several teams of corpsmen. Dead Marines were placed in black plastic bags that zipped up the front. Marine identification tags would be used back at An Hoa or at BUMED at Da Nang to identify the KIAs. The wounded Marines would be stabilized at the BAS (battalion aid station) at An Hoa and flown to Da Nang if their wounds were critical. Since most of the wounds were from gunshot, the severity of the injuries was presumed to be high.

The captain called for the report.

Gutierrez sensed the anticipation in the captain's voice. Battle statistics were always painful for the staff noncommissioned officers who led the troops into a fight. Hotel had lost some outstanding Marines on the sandbar island that morning. Many others would never be whole again. Not to mention the anxiety and emotional pain that resulted from seeing so many of their brothers make the final sacrifice.

Gunny reported, "We have fifty-seven enemy KIA. WIA unknown; no WIA bodies found. Friendly casualties: twelve U.S.M.C. KIA, forty-two WIA, thirty-two WIA evacuated. Enemy forces moving west to vicinity La Bac 1 and 2. Estimate one hundred fifty to two hundred enemy soldiers surviving artillery fire missions. Estimate fifty probable enemy WIA from weapons found and blood trails. Found three BARs, three K-44s, one carbine, two K-50s, one AK-47, one M-14, eighteen grenades, nine hundred rounds ammunition, three 82mm mortar rounds, four pounds documents."

The gunny then faced the troops of Third Platoon. They looked weary, and it was only 1300 hours. "Take fifteen minutes and get some chow down in your guts. We got a long day ahead of us yet."

Burns couldn't keep his mouth shut on a bet. "Hey, Lafley," he said, "do we gotta eat around all these dead fuckers? Jeez, the smell and all the flies and stuff is enough to ruin an appetite." Not many Marines appreciated Burns's humor that day. After the fight they had just been through, it would take some time before anything would seem funny. Most of the men smoked a cigarette, periodically glancing thoughtfully down at stained sand on the beach where the tattered remains of the dead and wounded still lay.

CHAPTER THIRTY

D Day Plus Two—
"Assault on La Bac 1
and 2"

The company commander was conferring with the platoon commanders of Hotel Company. Half a dozen officers and staff NCOs were huddled along the tree line, facing the trench line with its sprawl of enemy dead.

The commander directed the attention of his leaders to the west down the long stretch of road that led to the villages of La Bac 1 and 2. "Gentlemen, the Viet Cong have retreated in battle order down this road. They still have roughly half their force intact and are prepared to continue this engagement. The villages of La Bac 1 and 2 are the obvious defensive positions that the enemy will hold. Charlie has perhaps as many as fifty wounded soldiers that he has evacuated to the west. The troops in this trench line were a suicide squad of seriously wounded left to slow our advance. We must make another assault on La Bac Village to defeat the enemy and bring this campaign to a conclusion. Crimson Leader Actual wants a complete rout and destruction of the enemy forces. We have no available reserves for the assault. The final attack rests on our shoulders. Good luck! Third Platoon of Hotel will take the point. Foxtrot will cover our port flank, while the river will screen our starboard flank. I make it thirteen-twenty-five hours. Let's get the men saddled up and move out."

The platoon leaders stood and complied in standard Marine form: "Aye, aye, sir!"

Third Platoon's acting commander, Gunner Sergeant Gutierrez, returned to speak to the resting troops. "All right, men, let's get saddled up. Hamilton's squad will take the point into La Bac 1. There is still an enemy rifle company somewhere down that road. Foxtrot will be maneuvering on our port flank. Watch the direction of your rifle fire. Move out."

Burns and Lafley picked up the point positions in the double column, which straddled the road. The Marines marched in a staggered formation up the road to La Bac 1.

The road ahead of Lafley and Burns was intermittently shaded by the limbs of stately rows of trees that flanked both sides of the roadway. In the recent past in old Indochina, the road had led up the slight hill to a French plantation. Each Marine kept his eyes sweeping ahead along the edges of the fields bordering the road to La Bac 1. Large, fernlike plants grew to each side of the road in clumps that blocked visibility as the point Marines scanned the flanks for enemy movement.

I had cleaned the matted sand from the receiver of my M-14 during the pause at the top of the southern bank, after Hotel's crossing. I had poured a whole canteen of water over and into the receiver and open bolt mechanism. A few drops of oil on the bolt's camming surfaces and locking lug roller had gotten my rifle back into operation, and none too soon. As Lafley now rounded a wide bend in the road past a tight clump of trees, enemy shots rang out from a concealed position a hundred meters farther up the road.

The bullets missed the point fire team entirely, but several rounds hit the platoon's radio operator, walking just ahead of Gunny Gutierrez in the middle of the column. The radioman had taken the rounds in the torso, and as he hit the deck Marines were already pressing battle dressings over the bullet wounds in his rib cage and lower abdomen. The radioman's body slumped in his buddies' grasp, and his helmet slipped off his head. The inside of his helmet liner was covered with bone fragments, blood, and brain tissue, which protruded from the gaping bullet wound that had sliced the top off his skull, ending his young life.

The point Marines returned the fire and yelled back to the platoon commander that they had run into a sniper position. Gunny reacted immediately, and called to the rear for the 60mm mortar crew to bring their weapon forward.

Gunny gauged the distance from Lafley to the dirt mound ahead, from which the sniper fire had issued, at one hundred meters. "Culbertson," he ordered, "get up on the point and put some grazing fire into that bunker. Those boys on the 60mm mortar are too close to fire on that position."

I ran ahead in a low crouch, weaving toward Lafley and Burns, ahead on the side of the road. When I sighted Lafley, he motioned with his outstretched hand for me to get down. I fell into a prone position and sighted my rifle on the shallow berm in the field of camouflaging ferns. I had a twenty-round magazine in my weapon, and I clicked off the safety while sliding my cheek down along the wooden stock. The rifle sights came into alignment as I brought the front sight post into a six o'clock hold on the top of the bunker's front parapet. I took in a full breath and let half of it escape through my pursed lips. Holding the rest of my breath, I gradually took up the trigger slack until the rifle discharged and the round flew from the muzzle and slammed into the bunker, kicking a plume of dirt into the air. I let the muzzle rise a few inches, and when it settled I reacquired my six o'clock sight picture and broke another shot. It impacted cleanly into the hole the first bullet had made in the earth wall. By the time the magazine was exhausted a gaping hole a foot deep and eighteen inches wide had appeared in the front of the bunker. I reloaded, discarding the spent magazine and pulling the operating rod to the rear to chamber another round.

An enemy sniper poked his head, covered by a green canvas pith helmet, into the shallow space just above his parapet. I took a six o'clock sight picture at the Viet Cong's throat and broke the shot. The bullet caught the enemy sniper at the point of his chin and, fracturing his jaw, tore out the bottom row of teeth and exited, breaking his neck.

Tom Jiminez came up to my position. He held his M-79 grenade launcher casually. "Culbertson, how many dinks you got in that hole, man?"

"At least one more," I replied. Perhaps there were two left.

Jiminez shoved a 40mm grenade into the blooper and clicked the barrel shut the way you would a shotgun. He placed the wooden stock to his shoulder and estimated the yardage to his target. The weapon recoiled noticeably as the muzzle coughed, *thuuumph.* The round traced a shallow arc toward the enemy bunker. *Kaablaaam!* The 40mm round detonated just over the bunker, showering the Viet Cong inside the fighting hole with debris. The next round PFC Jiminez fired was aimed a fraction lower, and it slammed into the bunker's cavity after just clearing the front parapet. The explosion blew Charlie's lifeless form into the air above the dugout. Arms flailing wildly, the VC fell back to the bottom of his hole. The third sniper was wounded, but not intimidated. He fired a rapid volley of shots from the top of the berm. Then Lafley's point fire team exploded, and dozens of rounds slapped into the bunker and its last living occupant. The Viet Cong's dead body pitched into the rear of the fighting hole as he joined his two comrades in hell. The rough face of the bunker wall's wooden slats was painted in blood, and Charlie slipped down into a limp squat, oozing trickles of red from the dozen bullet holes that had stitched his lifeless trunk.

CHAPTER THIRTY-ONE

D Day Plus Two—
"Resistance in
La Bac 2"

First Squad of Hotel's Third Platoon walked around the edges of the snipers' bunker. The VC were lying in a contorted pile at the bottom. Arms and legs intertwined so that it was difficult to determine where one man ended and another began. They all wore green fatigue uniforms, rubber sandals, and green canvas cartridge belts loaded with ammunition and grenades. Green pith helmets with red star emblems on the front lay where they had tumbled off the dead soldiers' heads. Still within reach of the snipers' indifferent grasp, three weapons lay on the dirt floor of the bunker. Lafley pointed at one of the weapons. It was a long-barreled, wood-stocked, bolt-action weapon with a telescopic sight mounted on top of the polished receiver.

"That son of a bitch is mine!" he said. Lafley got on his knees and reached into the bunker to pluck out his prize. "This is a genuine Ruskie Moshin-Nagant sniper rifle. Burns and me saw plenty of 'em up on the

Z; ain't that right, Burns?" Lafley held out the rifle for the First Squad to feast their eyeballs on.

"This here is a 7.62-millimeter, bolt-action, highly accurate, flat-shooting son of a gun. The radio operator probably got plugged by this baby on that head shot. Well, that's the way it goes. War is hell!"

By then Gunny had reached the sniper bunker and was admonishing the men to spread out and keep moving toward La Bac 1. "What the hell are you girls gawkin' at? Haven't you ever seen dead gooks before? Get back on the fuckin' trail and spread it out. These three assholes are not the only enemy snipers in the area. Let's move out, Lafley and Burns! You two are starting to piss me off."

On that sour note, Lafley stepped up the pace, only to stop again and kneel down as the rumble of an explosion reached our ears. The cause of the blast was apparent when a sleek-bodied gray jet flared its flaps and dove over the far port tree line half a klick to our flank. The Phantom dropped a pair of black drumlike canisters off its wings before pulling up into a gentle climb and circling around for another attack. One after another, four F-4 Phantoms dived onto the target and released the black cylinders of jellied napalm. Black, tumbling billows laced with orange fire expanded into the gray afternoon sky. The great balls of black fire puffed themselves into monstrous shapes of swirling destruction. Everything in the path of the spreading napalm burst was consumed by the roiling turbulence of the hellfire.

The Foxtrot commander was on the radio to the lead F-4 to report that the enemy mortar had stopped firing. The point squad was taking heavy incoming automatic and rifle fire when the mortar began firing.

The F-4 leader said they were making another run armed with 250-pound contact bombs.

The jets had circled wide around the destroyed enemy mortar position. Enemy soldiers were observed in small groups running west along the main road toward the remaining Viet Cong main force body in La Bac 2. As the jets swung onto the approach for the bombing run, the pilots slowed the jets' descent as they homed in on their prey.

The bombs tumbled off their wing racks as the Phantoms pushed up their snouts to streak clear of the cone of spreading shrapnel fragments that would quickly tear into the landscape. The fourth jet dropped its ordnance and banked as Viet Cong soldiers raced into the shaded glens of the ancient French plantation. The 250-pound contact bombs slammed through the canopy of trees and burst in the midst of the fleeing Viet Cong. The clean air was transformed into a cauldron of choking black smoke and a wave of jagged shrapnel sliced the bark off the trees, the accompanying blast tossing the Viet Cong like toy soldiers and slicing their bodies with hot steel knives.

The F-4 leader reported the Phantoms would refuel and rearm, and be ready to scramble in one hour if further air support was required.

The Foxtrot commander ordered his platoons back into the assault. The lead squad of Foxtrot spread out into a line of skirmishers as they jogged through the remains of the French plantation amid the still-smoking bomb craters. The point fire teams glanced at the burned green-uniformed bodies of the enemy dead as they lay together in tortured clumps. As the Marines passed, swarms of flies rose off their trophies, only to light upon the dark pools of congealing liquid that bathed the dead. The Marine grunts faced to port and starboard, searching for live enemy.

CHAPTER THIRTY-TWO

D Day Plus Two—
"Main Force Survivors"

Lafley got the point squad of Hotel back on the main road, where they marched in twin columns along the road's edges. Their attention was still drawn to the F-4 attack along Foxtrot's line of advance. Black columns of smoke rose high in the afternoon sky for a thousand meters along the road to La Bac 2.

"Foxtrot must have run into some rough shit to need all that air support." Hamilton's opinion was offered to the squad at large.

Gary Woodruff broke into the analysis. "Remember that time up on the DMZ when those enemy mortar positions put the company on the deck for an hour? I'll bet a dollar to a dime the gooks had an 82mm mortar firing on that road junction."

"Hell, the Phantoms dropped enough ordnance to destroy the whole damn gook army up ahead there," Petersen said.

Gunny was up to the point squad again. "Lafley, put Culbertson on point and you and Burns cover his flanks. Foxtrot just jumped an enemy platoon armed with machine guns and mortars. Those F-4s tore

Charlie's ass up. There may be more surprises up ahead as we close on the village. Keep alert! Culbertson, fire on any movement to your immediate front. Is that clear?"

As the platoon fanned out through the plantation's rubber field, I had moved past Burns into the lead slot. "I am to fire on movement to my front. Aye, aye, Gunny." I was relatively new, and I repeated the order by the book.

"I will fire on any movement to my front, Gunny," Burns mimicked, just to my right rear. "You better fire into the gooks, 'cause those bastards are waiting for us up ahead. I promise you, rookie, you better keep your eyes peeled!"

We advanced a hundred meters farther up the trail, where I stopped the column. A large wooden hut of some kind loomed in the midst of the plantation about half a klick ahead. Its shape was hard to distinguish because of the trees surrounding it. As I rose to move ahead, shots rang out from the hut and the *crack* of bullets came low over the point squad's heads. Gunny was "up to the point" quickly, and crouched by my side. "Culbertson," he said, "you and Burns advance at the crawl up the trail until you are in firing range of that hut. I want you to pin those Viet Cong soldiers down while Matarazzi moves his gun onto your flank. PFC Jiminez will envelop the opposite flank and put M-79 fire into that hut. When Jiminez commences firing the gooks may try to bug out. If they make a run for alternate cover, Mat's gun can take care of that situation. Let's move out, Culbertson! Burns, watch his back!"

I fell onto my stomach, cradled my M-14 rifle in the crooks of my elbows, and began to low-crawl forward, toward the hut. Burns grunted to my rear as the rough terrain in the rubber tree field took its toll on our elbows and knees. Burns spoke first. "Culbertson," he said, "I make it about four hundred meters to that fuckin' hut. Can you hit the son of a bitch from here? My knees are killin' me."

I stretched out of the crawl position, and my weapon must have reflected a beam of sunlight. As Viet Cong bullets kicked up the grass and dirt in our faces, the hut was lit up by a series of bright muzzle flashes. I shouldered my weapon and sighted in at six o'clock under the flashes of the enemy guns. I took up the trigger slack and broke the first shot clean into the door of the hut. The rifle bucked, and I tightened my "spot weld," where my cheek embraced the stock, and rode the recoil. I picked up my sight alignment again at six o'clock. I fired round after round until the magazine was empty. I took a fresh magazine from the web pouch at my belt and, inserting it into my rifle's magazine well, I went back to work. By the time I had fired forty rounds into the hut, a black plume of smoke was twisting through the front door.

Matarazzi was near my port flank and had his gun set up, the ammo belt, gleaming in the sunlight, stretched long and deadly out the left side of the receiver. Mat yelled at me, "I don't see any movement. Let's wait and see if that fire gets going."

Within a few minutes, red flames licked from the windows of the hut and the smoke plume had become a cloud. Suddenly two shapes burst from the rear of the hut, zigzagging across the field and away from my position. I raised my rifle and sighted in on the leader. I led the Viet Cong a foot ahead of his left shoulder as he ran obliquely across my field of vision. At about 450 meters the enemy crossed my port flank toward Tom Jiminez. I squeezed the trigger gently, like plucking a fresh grape off the stem. The shot broke, and the Viet Cong pitched forward with a gaping hole in his left shoulder, where the bullet had entered his back. The Viet Cong struggled to his feet as Matarazzi squeezed the trigger on the M-60 machine gun.

A hail of bullets lit by the red burning streaks of tracers, every fifth round in the gun belt, impacted right around the two Viet Cong soldiers. The earth under their feet was pitched into the air, then the fusillade of steel laced into their bodies from head to foot, the soft green of their uniforms now stained with crimson.

Gunny was back up to the point squad again. He kneeled and examined the situation. "Let's go take a look at that hut before the damn thing burns to the ground. Culbertson, Burns, and the rest of First Squad, fan out and be prepared to fire if anything is alive in there."

The hut was already engulfed in flames and there was no way of determining how many enemy soldiers had been inside. Jiminez spoke up from the rear of the hut. "Gunny, they're out here. Three of 'em. Dead as a stringer of bass." We ran around the hut and there they lay. Three Viet Cong soldiers twisted into a pile. Ten feet outside the hut where they had been dragged by their comrades. Either dead or dying, they'd been abandoned when the hut was engulfed in flames.

Gunny spoke up as the exhausted troops of First Squad drank from their canteens. "Culbertson, you are doin' an outstanding job on point. I make it you got five clean kills this afternoon. First Squad gets credit for the first three dinks, plus these five, is eight enemy kills this afternoon not counting artillery. In fifteen minutes, we are moving up to the assault line to enter La Bac 1. The captain wants the village destroyed and everything in it killed. Before the assault waves move in, we will run artillery missions on La Bac 1 and 2. Once we are into the village, do not hesitate to fire upon anything that moves. This area is clearly Viet Cong territory, and there are no friendly villagers in the vicinity. That is all."

CHAPTER THIRTY-THREE

D Day Plus Two—
"The Second Assault—
La Bac 1"

First Squad knelt at the edge of the last tree line that separated the old plantation from the village of La Bac. In colonial times, La Bac must have supplied the cheap labor that annually extracted the rubber latex from the thousands of trees on the plantation. The fields were laid in neat squares surrounding a dilapidated French colonial mansion with screened porches that provided a 360-degree panorama of the rich fields.

La Bac 1, on the other hand, appeared to be another ville of thatch-roofed, dirt-floor hootches, a common village with no outstanding features—except that La Bac 1 was now occupied by the desperate remnant of the R-20th Viet Cong Main Force Battalion. Along with the wounded and dying soldiers that the Viet Cong had carried to La Bac Village during their retreat from the Song Thu Bon trench line, the Communists still fielded a hundred able fighting men. They were still well provisioned with ammunition and food supplies. They would not turn La Bac over to the Marines without another fight.

This time the Marines softened up La Bac with a dose of artillery fire before the troops moved in to the assault. Gunny got on the hook to FSCC An Hoa and ordered a fire mission preparatory to the assault.

In the far distance, a single gun boomed into the late-afternoon sky toward the agricultural paradise of Arizona. The round reached its zenith and nosed earthward, picking up velocity as it fell toward the uncomfortable quiet of La Bac 1.

Whaaam! The smoke trails announced to the Marines and the enemy that another artillery mission would arrive soon with all its deadly power directed at the flimsy huts of La Bac 1.

Immediately the Viet Cong soldiers in La Bac crept into tunnels that slanted down into massive domed bunkers under the village. There they would wait out the fury of the barrage. Then they would scurry to the surface to take up positions in spider holes and slit trenches flanked by the protective shadows of the huts.

Gunny picked up the radio handset to call for fire, requesting high-explosive delayed fuses. Gunny wasn't naive. He knew Charlie would be in his bunkers. High-explosive delayed fuses had worked wonders back at the river trench line. Gunny saw no reason to change strategy at this point.

The big guns at An Hoa boomed in sequence, sending huge smoke rings into the air that expanded as they billowed away from the muzzles. The four rounds of the salvo fell mercilessly on their prey. The rounds impacted on the dirt square, penetrating into the solid bunkers housing the main force battalion. Thick beams split into shards as the huge shells pierced the underground cavities and exploded in the darkness. The explosions were muffled underground by the tons of earth and wood covering the huge bunkers. One bunker received a direct hit from two rounds.

Half of the Viet Cong soldiers were killed or seriously wounded by the four salvos of 155mm howitzer fire that fell on La Bac 1. The survivors gamely climbed from their bunkers and assumed firing positions in the trenches and holes spaced among the burning huts. Their fate already sealed, the remnants of R-20th Main Force Battalion waited with a handful of North Vietnamese advisers who had also escaped the barrage.

As the last shells of the fourth fire mission blew geysers of dirt and straw thatch into the air over La Bac 1, Gunny Gutierrez got on the radio and terminated the fire support.

Gunny reported in to the company radio net for authority to order the assault from his commanding officer. The company commander had just ordered Hotel's two trailing platoons forward to support the assault once the guns started booming in An Hoa at FSCC.

Gunny motioned to Hamilton, who had formed his squad into the first assault line. "Hamilton," he commanded, "advance to the front of that first line of huts and assume firing positions. Gedzyk will have his gun set up on your starboard flank, firing into the huts before you assault. Let's move out and finish the stragglers. Most of 'em have got to be wounded after the artillery missions."

Luther motioned his squad forward over the rubble-strewn road heading into the village's main row of burning huts. Gedzyk's gun commenced firing on our flank. The impacts of the machine gun bullets splintered the flimsy walls of the huts, tearing gaping holes that revealed sparsely furnished interiors. Hamilton's Marines assumed firing positions and on command poured a volley of grazing fire into the burning hell of La Bac 1.

The firing let up after a few short minutes. The devastation that the Marine bullets had wrought was unbelievable. Corpses were draped across doorways and littered the street that wound through the village. Hamilton turned to his squad and yelled, "Get on line, you bastards. Move into the village. Fire at will!"

The squad moved slowly forward to the steady pounding of rifles. Not more than twenty paces to the rear, the second and third squads followed, ready to fill the gaps should any of the Marines in the first squad fall to enemy fire.

The first Viet Cong spider hole opened under a woven winnowing mat. The wounded enemy soldier popped up and took careful aim at a trooper bringing up the first squad's flank. *Blam! Blaam! Blaam!* The SKS semiautomatic rifle spit. The young Marine on the flank faltered, then pitched forward—another "new guy," this one had lasted less than a month. It was the seasoned troopers like Lafley, Burns, Ybarra, and Jessmore who were hard to kill—or just damn lucky.

Burns wheeled in the street to face a row of huts, then called to Lafley. "Watch my back. I'm going into that hut and see what's left alive." He entered the smoking frame of the doorway. Screams became audible as the staccato rhythm of Burns's rifle silenced the noise. Burns emerged wearing a Viet Cong pith helmet, the red star shining in the front.

Burns rejoined the squad. "Take off that fuckin' hat, you maniac," Lafley said. "Somebody's gonna cap your ass if they see that." Lafley reached up and grabbed the helmet and tucked it under his arm. The Marines had fanned out inside the village, and rifle fire was exploding into every spider hole and dugout as Viet Cong soldiers were cut down where they fought. In the far corners of the burning village, unseen and unheard Viet Cong soldiers were slipping into the shadows, running from the confusion into the safety of the jungle.

The dozen Viet Cong left behind died in their holes. The wounded Communist troops fought valiantly to the death, since no hope of escape was left for them. The Marines of Red Platoon "fired them up." The village had been cleared of its defenders thirty minutes after the action began. Only one Marine had been killed and several more wounded. One trooper had been seriously wounded when he searched a dead Viet Cong who held a live grenade "safely" in his death grasp. The movement of his cold limbs had released the spoon and detonated the charge. The Marine took the bulk of the shrapnel in his flak jacket, but some of the wire shards of the M-26 grenade had cut into his exposed face and blinded him.

As Hamilton's troops secured the village and rechecked every hootch, Gunny was on the radio to the company commander in the rear with White Platoon.

The company commander had seen the fighting from the reserve platoon's firing line, but had not witnessed the destruction up close.

Gunny and the troopers of Third Platoon slumped against the charred huts of La Bac 1 and savored a cigarette. Every man had fought continuously for over nine hours as the R-20th Main Force Battalion and its North Vietnamese cadre had been savaged in two frontal assaults by the Marines of Foxtrot and Hotel and their supporting arms. Every Marine would remember forever the bloodstained sandbar littered with dead and dying brother Marines, cut down before their time.

The handset squelched as the battalion commander came up on the net for Gunny.

"Crimson Two Red Leader, this is Crimson Leader Actual. Congratulations on outstanding performance by Red Platoon today. Crimson Two Actual confirms nineteen enemy KIAs. Extend my highest regards to the troops. Battalion will honor Crimson Two with more fitting ceremony upon return to An Hoa. Permission granted to stand down the men. *Semper fidelis!* Crimson Leader Actual. Out."

Epilogue

D Day Plus Four

The gunnery sergeant passed the word to Hotel's point platoon to stand down for the day. They had driven the remaining enemy soldiers into the jungle. The blocking forces had called air strikes on the hills surrounding their positions. No further contact of any appreciable size was made during the next two days of Operation TUSCALOOSA as the Marines of H&S, Foxtrot, and Hotel companies swept back toward An Hoa.

On January 27, 1967, the point platoon of Foxtrot Company encountered twelve enemy soldiers. The platoon pursued by fire and pushed the enemy into the open, where an air strike was run. A scout sniper team from Foxtrot accounted for one enemy KIA.

Later in the day on January 27, a fresh rifle company was helilifted into the vicinity of Le Nam 3. The Marines of Delta Company, First Battalion, Twenty-sixth Marine Regiment swept northwest. Delta Company Marines received 35 rounds of enemy automatic weapons fire at 1230 hours on January 28. Company D returned fire with 650 rounds of rifle and automatic weapons, 20 rounds of M-79, and 44 rounds of 105mm howitzer fire, then pursued the enemy into high ground. The men of Delta then searched the area, finding blood trails. Unable to reestablish contact, Delta Company marched to Phu Loc 6. At 1800 hours Delta Company was helilifted to Twenty-sixth Marines Battalion CP at Da Nang.

On January 27, the commanding general of the First Marine Division visited the Second Battalion, Fifth Marines command post at Phu Loc 6. Operation TUSCALOOSA was officially terminated at 1800 hours on January 28, 1967.

The officers of the Second Battalion of the Fifth Marine Regiment were standing at parade rest behind their battalion commander, facing the weathered profile of the commanding general as he addressed the assemblage.

"Gentlemen, I want to salute the commanding officer of the Two-Five, Colonel Airheart. His staff and company officers have performed magnificently in the face of overwhelming obstacles. Two-Five took the field on short notice and faced off with a veteran main force battalion numbering over three hundred and fifty regulars with twenty or more North Vietnamese officers and NCOs serving as advisers. The river assaults conducted by Foxtrot and Hotel were textbook exercises, and illustrated the time-honored courage of U.S. Marines under fire. The enemy was pursued and eliminated in his fighting holes across the La Bac plantation plateau. The second assault of the day produced significant results in reducing the enemy's will to fight. The enemy strength was reduced to a platoon in the village of La Bac. The fleeing enemy soldiers carried dead and wounded into the jungle with them. It is safe to say that the R-20th Main Force Battalion ceased to exist as a fighting arm of the Viet Cong by sixteen hundred hours on January 26, 1967.

"Casualties are confirmed officially as: enemy, seventy-nine KIA confirmed, sixty-four KIA probable, twenty-eight WIA confirmed, fifty WIA probable. Friendly casualties are: USMC seventeen KIA confirmed, USN two KIA, thirty-eight WIA evacuated, fourteen WIA nonevacuated.

"The Marines of Two-Five have killed or wounded two hundred and twenty-one enemy soldiers in four days of battle. That is outstanding! Gentlemen, the Marines will always have a purpose—to attack and destroy the enemies of the United States of America. Gentlemen, please raise your glasses in salute to the victors of the Second Battalion, Fifth Marines and to their commanding officer. None finer!"

On cue, the officers of the Second Battalion, Fifth Marines clicked their boot heels together in unison. Their glasses of whiskey and beer were raised toward the commanding general, who beamed in satisfaction. In one voice the officers honored the fallen.

"None finer!"

Glossary

A-4 Sky Raider—Single-engine U.S.M.C. attack jet. Medium size and subsonic.

Actual—The commander of a platoon, company, battalion, etc.

AK-47—Main VC fully automatic battle rifle in 7.62 × 39mm.

Ambush—A covert attack method employed by both VC and Marines by firing on an unawares enemy from seclusion, often employing booby traps or mines.

Amtrac—Marine tracked armored personnel carrier, troops loaded through rear ramp door.

An Hoa—The ancient French fortress that comprised the westernmost logistical base of the Marines. Thirty miles southwest of Da Nang.

Arizona—The rice paddy territory of Dai Loc and Duc Duc provinces in South Vietnam stretching west and southwest from Da Nang.

Arty—Artillery used in fire support missions.

ARVN—Army of the Republic of South Vietnam.

Assault line—Marine attack formation with troops advancing abreast.

AT—Artillery target coordinates giving exact map locations on U.S.M.C. topographical maps.

Azimuth—Compass heading toward an objective or target.

Back azimuth—180° opposite compass heading to an azimuth. This points to where a patrol has been.

Ball, ammo—F.M.J. (full metal jacket), usually weighing 150 grains in 7.62 × 51mm standard NATO bullet.

Bandolier—A linked belt of machine gun ammo often worn across the chest.

Battalion—A Marine combat unit composed of four rifle companies and a headquarters company.

Battle dressing—A rectangular three-by-five-inch (approximate size) medical dressing carried into combat by Marines.

Betel nut—Narcotic seed nut chewed by Vietnamese villagers that colors teeth and gums blood red.

Blue Leader—The radio code of the first platoon commander of Hotel Company.

Boondocks, boonies—The jungle or bush outside An Hoa's perimeter.

Boots, jungle—Special canvas tops attached to lightweight leather boots with steel-shank protective soles.

Bouncing betty—A U.S. mine that pops into the air at waist level when triggered before detonation.

Cap—To "cap" an enemy is to bust a "primer cap" when firing a weapon at Charlie. To kill an enemy.

CH-46—Sea Knight helicopter, capable of lifting a rifle platoon. Twin engines.

Charlie—Victor Charlie, the South Vietnamese Communist soldier and the Marine's main foe in the Arizona.

Checkpoint—1. Any number of sentry-guarded entrances to An Hoa Combat Base; 2. The exact positions on a topographical map that a Marine patrol must intersect and radio in to headquarters.

Chi-com—Any weapon or explosive manufactured by the Chinese Communists.

Chieu hoi—A term used by VC or North Vietnamese to proclaim their unconditional surrender.

Chow—Marine slang for mealtime, or to eat "chow."

Claymore—Directional mine armed with plastic explosive and a ball-bearing-studded face. Antipersonnel defensive mine.

Click, klick—A unit of distance equal to 1,000 linear meters. Commonly used gauge for estimating distance in artillery-compatible gradations. One kilometer.

Clip—Marine slang for "to cut down" with rifle fire.

C-Med—Charlie Medical Facility at Da Nang. A surgical unit.

CO—Commanding officer.

Colonel—The commander of Second Battalion, Fifth Marine Regiment. Actually, his rank is lieutenant colonel, but in the field colonel is used exclusively.

Concertina—A circular rolled barbed or razor wire used in constructing a perimeter defense.

CP—Marine command post.

C rations—The standard U.S. government canned meal, ready to eat in the field.

Crimson Leader Actual—The radio call sign of the battalion commander of the 2/5.

Dai Loc—Province in the Arizona.

Da Nang—The giant Marine base and seaport on the China Sea, thirty miles north of An Hoa at the inception of Highway One.

Deck—The floor or ground. "Hit the deck" is a command to get down, usually under fire.

Defilade—A cut or low spot in the ground. Used as cover and concealment.

Delayed fuse—Artillery shells or bombs with delayed fuses that penetrate the ground before exploding.

Demo—Demolitions, usually C-4 plastic explosive. To "demo" a tunnel is to blow it up.

Deploy—To order troops into a specific battle formation.

Deputy—The deputy commander of the First Marine Division was a brigadier general.

Di di mau—"Run away" or "escape" in Vietnamese.

Dike—A built-up wall with a footpath above a surrounding rice field. Dikes are roads for the rice farmer.

Dink—A Vietnamese or Viet Cong (dinky).

Division—In Vietnam the U.S.M.C. fielded the First, Third, and Fifth divisions. Each division is composed of three regiments. The Fifth Marine Regiment was part of the First Division. The Twenty-sixth Marines were part of the Fifth Division.

DMZ—Or the Z. The demilitarized zone dividing North and South Vietnam.

Doc—Medical personnel or corpsman.

Duc Duc—Rice basin north of An Hoa Combat Base.

Dung lai—To halt or order to stop in Vietnamese.

Enfilade fire—Rifle or machine gun fire from a 45-degree angle from either front cutting across a position.

Envelop (right or left)—A tactic where a flanking fire team or squad encircles the enemy on its periphery while a base squad maintains fire superiority.

Evasion—Tactics used by the VC to avoid contact with Marine patrols.

F-4—A twin-engine jet fighter/bomber used by Marine air wings for ground support for infantry units. The McDonnell Douglas F-4 Phantom.

Field—The field is any area outside the main base where combat readiness is mandatory.

Field of fire—The radius that an automatic weapon can cover in an arc from port to starboard.

Firebase—Phu Loc 6 was the main artillery support base and Marine-guarded hill at the entrance to the Arizona some six miles north of An Hoa.

Firefight—An engagement of small units employing mainly rifle fire and small arms.

Fire in the hole!—The correct exclamation or preparatory warning before discharging explosives. A warning shouted when tripping a booby trap or mine.

Fire mission—An artillery mission fired to support troops in the field, or H and I fire.

Firepit—Artillery revetments to segregate guns to lessen fire hazards.

Fire team—The basic building block of the Marine rifle squad. A fire team contains a leader, two riflemen, and an automatic rifleman (M-14 with selector). A squad contains three fire teams.

Flag officer—A U.S. Marine general officer.

Flak jacket—The fiberglass-paneled cloth jacket (vest) worn by Marines as protection from shrapnel.

Flank—The side of a unit, where it is weakest.

FO—An artillery forward observer, who can adjust artillery fires onto a target.

Foxtrot—A sister company to Hotel. In the Second Battalion, Fifth Marines there are four rifle companies: E (Echo), F (Foxtrot), G (Golf), and H (Hotel).

Frag—Fragmentation grenade. The U.S. M-26 grenade was the standard fragmentation grenade. The U.S. M-34 was made with white phosphorus ("Willy Peter").

G-2—Intelligence division of a Marine divisional staff. The intelligence officer is the G-2 billet.

Garbled—Radio communication that is indecipherable.

Golf—A sister company in 2/5.

Go Noi Island—A main force headquarters in the Arizona on the Song Thu Bon to the northeast of An Hoa.

Grazing fire—Flat-trajectory rifle or machine gun fire aimed low to the deck against bunkered enemy troops.

Grid square—An area on a topographical map comprising 1,000 meters and defined by four coordinates. Six coordinates define the area to 100 square meters. Eight coordinates to 10 meters.

Groundpounders—Infantry troops. Grunts.

Grunt—Slang term for Marine infantry troops.

Gung ho—Marine spirit and enthusiasm.

H-34—Sikorksy UH-34 resupply and medevac chopper, used as the main Marine workhorse.

Halozone—Water-purification tablet.

Ham and motherfuckers—The most reviled C ration meal, which you could not give away—even to the dinks.

Hamlet—Small village in the Arizona with less than 100 population.

Hawk—Very cold climate or high wind.

H and I—Harassment and interdiction artillery fire. Sometimes called "we don't give a shit what we hit" fire. Designed to alter and hamper enemy movement.

HE—High-explosive shell or bomb.

Honcho—Native leader or village hetman.

Hot area—Dangerous, enemy-controlled landing zone strafed by enemy fire.

Hotel—Company in the 2/5.

HQ—Headquarters. The 2/5's HQ was at An Hoa. The First Marine Division's HQ was at Da Nang.

Hump—To walk a long distance on patrol or operation, usually loaded down with ammo and gear.

Incendiary—A shell that burns upon impact. White phosphorus shell.

Inchon—South Korean port where the First Marine Brigade made a historic landing.

Incoming fire—An enemy round of artillery or mortar round fired into a U.S.M.C. position.

Infiltration route—One of the network of trails used by North Vietnamese troops to enter South Vietnam from the north, Laos, or Cambodia.

Illumination—Night artillery fire used to illuminate an area using a phosphorus filament suspended by parachute.

Indian territory—Hostile area controlled by enemy forces.

K-44—Chinese Communist battle rifle.

K-bar—World War II–vintage U.S.M.C. combat knife.

KC-130—Main U.S. Air Force transport plane with four engines and rear ramp loading. Carries a combat-ready rifle platoon.

KIA—Killed in action.

Kit Carson Scout—An NVA soldier who defected and scouted for Marine patrols.

Kwajalein—South Pacific atoll assaulted by Marines in World War II.

Land mine—Various types were constructed by the VC, especially utilizing undetonated U.S. bombs.

LAW—Light Antitank Weapon, contained in collapsible, disposable, fiberglass tubes.

Liberty Bridge—Linked An Hoa to firebase Phu Loc 6 across the Song Thu Bon some six miles north of An Hoa in the Arizona.

LP—Listening post or sentry post, fielded at night to provide warning of an enemy attack.

LZ—Landing zone for helicopters.

M-1—World War II main battle rifle. Air-cooled, clip-fed, semiautomatic, shoulder-held rifle in caliber .30 MI. Occasionally used by VC and stolen from the ARVN. Arguably the finest battle rifle ever fielded by the United States.

M-1/M-2 .30-caliber carbine—U.S. air-cooled, magazine-fed, shoulder-held, World War II–vintage carbine, .30 caliber. Favorite weapon of officers and South Vietnamese due to light weight. The M-2 version is fully automatic.

M-2 . 50-caliber machine gun—U.S. air-cooled, belt-fed, fully automatic, pylon- or tripod-mounted heavy machine gun, .50 caliber.

M-14—The standard U.S.M.C. main battle rifle. Air-cooled, magazine-fed, shoulder-held, semiautomatic rifle in 7.62mm NATO.

M-26—The standard U.S. fragmentation grenade with coiled wire filament-encased fragmentation spool.

M-60 machine gun—U.S. air-cooled, belt-fed, fully automatic, shoulder-fired standard infantry machine gun, 7.62mm NATO, with bipod and replacement barrels.

M-60 tank—Main U.S. battle tank, equipped with 90mm main gun and .50- and .30-caliber machine guns. Weight: 58 tons, approximately.

M-72—Light Antitank Weapon (LAW) rocket. A plastic tube extended to fire a shaped, charged rocket that would penetrate eleven inches of concrete or heavy logged bunkers. Replaced 3.5-inch rocket launcher.

M-79—U.S. shoulder-held, 40mm, single-shot grenade launcher with range around 400 meters.

III MAF—Marine Amphibious Force. The senior headquarters of Marine operations in Vietnam's I Corps area. Troop strength was eighteen infantry battalions.

MAG—Marine Air Group.

Mamma-san—The older mothers and grandmothers in a peasant village.

Medevac—Medical evacuation, usually by H-34 helicopter, although CH-46 Sea Knights were used on TUSCALOOSA.

MG—Designation for machine gun.

MIA—Missing in action.

Mike Mike—The radio code for artillery piece defined by caliber in millimeters. Example: 155 Mike Mike is a 155-millimeter howitzer.

Mortars—U.S. mortars are 60mm portable mortar, 81mm mortar used in the field only from fixed positions, and 4.2-inch mortar fired from firebase at Phu Loc 6. The main VC mortar was the 82mm Chinese infantry weapon.

Moshin nagant—Russian bolt-action rifle in 7.62mm, of World War II vintage.

MOS—Military Occupational Specialty, or job description. Marine infantry was 0300. A rifleman was 0311.

Napalm—Jellied gasoline in canisters dropped from jets. Sucked all available oxygen into its fireball.

Net—Radio network.

Number one—Vietnamese slang for "the best."

Number ten—Vietnamese slang for "the worst."

NVA—North Vietnamese Army regular soldiers.

Ontos—Marine tracked attack vehicle sporting six
                106mm recoilless rifles and .50-caliber
                spotting rifle.

OP—Observation post.

OPCON—Operational Control. Delta 1-26 was
                OPCON to 2/5 during Tuscaloosa on
                January 27–28, 1967.

Paddy—The rectangular rice fields bordered by dikes
                and footpaths.

PF—Popular Forces, the Vietnamese National Guard.

Plunging fire—Rifle and machine gun fire aimed
                down onto target from a position higher
                than the enemy.

Point—Lead Marine in a rifle squad on patrol. Lead
                element in a company column.

Point detonating fuses—Shells or bombs that explode
                on impact.

Police—To clean up or sanitize.

Probe—To attack a defensive perimeter line to ana-
                lyze weapon placement.

Punji stake—A sharpened bamboo stake smeared with
                excrement and/or urine.

Racks—Bomb racks, where aviation ordnance is hung
                on the aircraft underwing or belly;
                Marine slang for bunk or bed.

R and R—Rest and relaxation. A short-term leave from combat duty.

Rear area—The combat base or any secure area outside the Arizona.

Recoilless rifle—The 106mm rifles on the Ontos fired perforated cased shells that blew the gases out the rear breech ports, reducing recoil.

Recon—To patrol looking for enemy movements in order to collect information. Recon patrols avoid combat if possible.

Red Leader—The radio code name for the Second Platoon commander of Hotel Company.

Regiment—U.S.M.C. unit composed of three rifle battalions and a headquarters. The 2/5 was a rifle battalion in the Fifth Marine Regiment.

Repeat—Radio fire mission coordinates and important facts are often repeated for clarity.

Seabees—U.S. Navy combat construction workers. They built the airstrip and most of the base at An Hoa.

Sea Knight—The CH-46 helicopter used for troop insertion and medevac on Operation TUSCALOOSA.

Scuttlebutt—Rumors or unfounded facts passed between Marines.

Short round—An artillery shell fired short of the target. This is a grave danger when firing over a unit of Marines toward the enemy.

Short-timer—A Marine with less than sixty days
        remaining in-country.

Skirmishers—A frontal attack formation with the
        squad in staggered line.

SKS—Simonov Soviet- or Chinese-made semiauto-
        matic 7.62×39mm rifle. This is the
        standard VC infantry weapon and is
        accurate and reliable.

Slack—Any easy treatment by the Marines toward
        anyone. This seldom happened.

Snuffie—A private enlisted Marine.

Spider hole—An enemy fighting hole camouflaged to
        the eye.

Square away—To make orderly and neat, specifically
        uniforms and equipment.

TAOR—Tactical area of responsibility, or battalion
        operational area.

TO—Table of organization.

Topo—Topographical map showing elevation of hills,
        valleys, and contour lines.

Top sergeant—First sergeant or senior enlisted man in
        a rifle company.

Trail—A well-used path linking villages or leading
        through the jungle. Often mined or
        booby-trapped.

Utilities—Green Marine combat uniform made of
        lightweight cotton. In Vietnam, combat
        utilities were called "jungles."

Vaporize—To blow an enemy to pieces.

VC—Viet Cong soldier.

Volley fire—When an entire Marine squad or platoon fires in rhythmical cadence together.

Waste—To kill without mercy.

WP—White phosphorus artillery shell or grenade.

White Leader—The radio code name of the Second Platoon commander of Hotel Company.

XO—Executive officer, second in command of a rifle company or battalion.

XRAY—Letter *X* in radio call signs.

Zap—To shoot or hit with a bullet.

Zero—To bring a rifle's sights into alignment at two hundred meters for accurate battle dope.

Zilch—Nothing, no luck.

SIX SILENT MEN
Book One
by Reynel Martinez

In 1965, when the 1st Brigade of the 101st Airborne Division was assigned to Vietnam, its staff quickly discovered that the only way to locate the enemy was to insert teams of six well-armed men into the jungle and let them look for him. *Six Silent Men* is the harrowing story of one of the earliest LRRP units, men whose trial by fire in the jungles of Vietnam is told here by one of their own.

Published by Ivy Books.
Available in bookstores everywhere.